Freedom*Shift*

Freedom*Shift*

3 Choices to Reclaim America's Destiny

Oliver DeMille

Freedom*Shift*: 3 Choices to Reclaim America's Destiny
Oliver DeMille

For information, contact info@thesocialleader.com.

Nothing in this work is prescriptive or intended as legal,
medical or other advice, and readers should consult competent
professionals about decisions.

Published 2010 in the United States of America
Published by The Center for Social Leadership,
www.thesocialleader.com

For wholesale and bulk discounts, contact sales@tjed.org.

Cover design by Charfish Design
Typeset and illustration by Daniel Ruesch Design

ISBN 978-1-4507-2879-9

"...the greatness of America lies not in being
more enlightened than any other nations,
but rather in her ability to repair her faults."

–Alexis de Tocqueville,
author of *Democracy in America*

Contents

The Future of Freedom

**Three things will change everything!
What are they, and how can we implement them?**

Americans enjoy a legacy of freedom and prosperity that is perhaps without equal in the history of the world. The pride we have traditionally felt over the idealism, vision, heroism, and sacrifice of our Pilgrims, Founders, and those that followed them is a part of our national heritage.

And yet it seems that it is no longer alarmist to assert that we are in grave danger of losing the freedom and prosperity that were won at so terrible a cost. Strangely, though, our culture of idealism, heroism and sacrifice is not lost.

Our people still show a great capacity for moral courage, tenacity and altruism. There are still those among us who are willing to take risks, endure hardships and make difficult choices. We still take our hats off when the flag goes by. We honor the sacrifices of our military brothers and sisters; we show compassion to the less fortunate. Why, then, are we sliding virtually unchecked down the slippery slope of cultural and societal decay?

Why are we losing our freedoms?

Santayana warns that a people that forgets is destined to repeat history. We have forgotten the great stories of how our freedom was won and the principles that they teach. Americans who are so demonstrably willing to labor and sacrifice for the benefit of their posterity can only allow the destruction of the forms that protect our freedoms if they do not understand what freedom is, nor how to maintain it.

A Freedom*Shift* is needed today. And to accomplish it I propose The Three Choices to Reclaim America's Destiny. Can it be possible that such a peaceful revolution can come from three simple choices made by a relative few?

Margaret Mead has been oft-quoted: "Never doubt that a small group of thoughtful, committed citizens can change the world. Indeed, it is the only thing that ever has."[1] Sometimes a few small and simple things sway everything, like the straw that breaks the camel's back. Malcolm Gladwell called this a tipping point, and in science it is called Disparate Distribution. In 1800 economist J.B. Say coined the term *entrepreneur* to describe those who drive the economy, and defined it with Say's Law: Entrepreneurs are the significant minority who take resources from unproductive places and make them productive.

History calls it "The Law of the Vital Few"; in math it is reflected in Factor Sparcity. In economics, the idea that small things guide the big things is often referred to as the 80-20 Rule or Pareto's Law. This concept asserts that 20% of our actions create 80% of the results and 20% of the people have 80% of the impact.

Some authors have written entire books declaring that the 80-20 Rule should really be called the 90-10 rule—that these numbers are closer to reality. Successful leaders even suggest that the 80-20 Rule is more accurately the 97-3 Rule: Three percent of the population controls 97% of the wealth, and three percent of any group or organization typically accounts for 97% of its success.

While "individual results may vary," the principle of the few swaying the many is a dynamic reality. This has been understood since ancient times, when the Greeks believed that if you had even one true warrior in a group of soldiers, they would be virtually impossible to beat. From David *versus* the Philistines to Gideon and his fighting band, the Hebrews canonized the story of God prospering his people in battle with only a very small army—selected from a larger one. It was the Chinese who first noted that very small rudders steer the largest of ships.

More recently, American founder John Adams philosophized at length regarding the dynamics of influence within a body of individuals. He asserted that in any group of one hundred human beings—regardless of race, culture or status—within a short period of time, most will choose to watch and be swayed, a few will rally sides and compete for prominence, and less than a handful will actually determine the course of action.[2]

One quaint and poetic way of teaching this principle is to say that when the world has great needs, God sends a baby to grow up and solve it. Indeed the impact of great men and women is hugely powerful—much more than you would expect from any one person. Consider the influence of an Einstein, a Gandhi, a Washington – Alexander, Caesar, Mother Teresa, and so on. It may be arguable that the 80-20 Rule applies within the context of economics, mathematics or business; but in the history of human greatness, certainly the 97-3 Rule prevails.

The "Great Books"[3] had much more impact on the development of human civilization than most of the mountains of books written through history, and Mortimer Adler argued that of all the ideas of humanity, a sparse few of them (which he called "The Great Ideas") had incredible sway.

My mentor Cleon Skousen reminded me dozens of times that during the American founding era a mere three percent of the population made most of the sacrifices, did most of the work and made the major decisions which established America as the most free and prosperous nation in history. This list could go on and on. Clearly: some significant small things greatly impact everything else.

Today, in our world of challenges and times of crises, *Who* are the three percent? And at least as important: *What* are the 3 Choices to Reclaim America's Destiny?

The Three Choices

For meaningful and lasting change to take place, we must first clearly identify and articulate the problems. If we allow as an assumption that freedom, prosperity and self-determination are universal human values, then we can measure American culture and the developing societal climate by these standards. With such a benchmark, there are at least three prevailing forces in the national paradigm that militate against these governing values. They are:

1. The Dominance of the Employee Mentality

2. The Two-Party Political Monopoly

3. The Industrial-Materialistic-Nationalized Mindset

The following chapters will explain how each of these does deep and serious harm to freedom, prosperity, families and happiness. Also defined and illustrated will be *The Three Choices*: three critical changes that can profoundly and positively shift our society in the right direction. Accomplish The Three Choices —or even one or two of them—and the resulting Freedom*Shift* will be a catalytic change that will reconfigure our societal landscape and reshape our prospects for the future. The Three Choices are:

1. A Revolution of Entrepreneurship

2. The Rise of the Independents

3. Building and Leading the New Tribes

Political parties, big business and the media misunderstand, underestimate or ignore The Three Choices, and regular citizens and future generations stand to suffer the consequences. It is time for regular Americans, and others who support freedom around the world, to understand The Three Choices. When we do, expect a tectonic Freedom*Shift* of progress to sweep the nation and beyond.

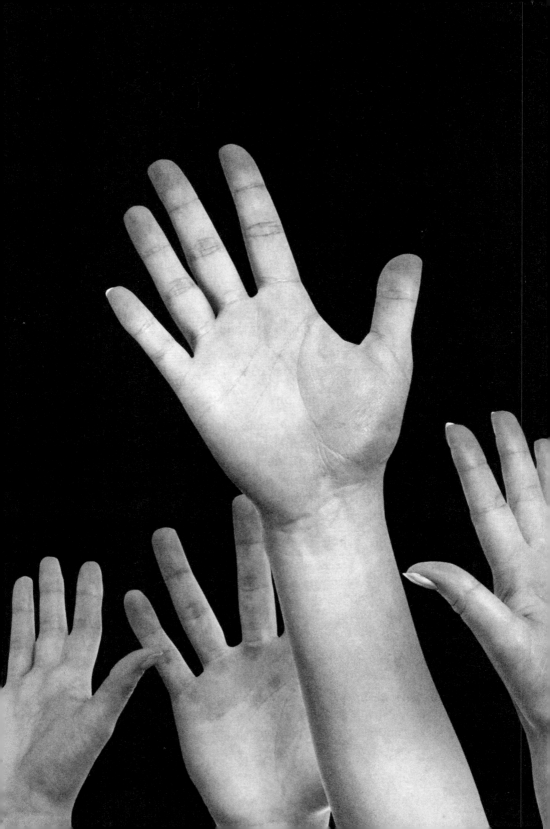

A Revolution of Entrepreneurship

Producers make things, build things, and create a better world. Sometimes called owners or entrepreneurs or leaders, producers see the world differently than those with a victim, employee or dependent mentality. Over time, fewer and fewer Americans are producers.

The resulting problem is less freedom.

The solution, vital to the future of freedom, is to have more producers.

CHAPTER

1

The Needed Revolution

It is time for a revolution. Not just any revolution—but a specific kind of Freedom*Shift* that will make the critical difference. We need a renaissance of the entrepreneurial mentality and many millions of entrepreneurs in our society. Whether by will or by force, the changes brought on by the recession of 2008 helped increase awareness of this need, and impelled many to take their professional and financial fate into their own hands. It stands to reason that a society populated by an increasing number of individuals who are taking responsibility for their own prosperity and security will, in the aggregate, become more prosperous and secure.

Jefferson praised the citizens who formed the foundation of a free society, contributing through their agriculture or manufacture. These independents not only took responsibility for and provided for themselves and their employees, but their surplus was "the sacred fund of the helpless poor." He further noted:

> "We remark with special satisfaction those [favorable circumstances] which, under the smiles of Providence, result from the skill, industry and order of our citizens managing their own affairs in their own way and for their own use, unembarrassed by too much regulations, unoppressed by fiscal exactions."

While much has changed in the two hundred years since Jefferson's day, the principles behind these sentiments are not outdated.

Our society's producers may be "embarrassed by regulations" and "oppressed by fiscal extractions;" however, the Information Age also affords some advantages for today's entrepreneurs.

And yet, these advantages of advanced technology and readily accessible information are not enough. Indeed, it has been said that for all the opportunity afforded us by this Age of Information, we are largely drowning in a sea of irrelevance. Social commentator Neil Postman warned of the gathering wave in his 1985 book, *Amusing Ourselves to Death*:

> "What [George] Orwell feared were those who would ban books. What [Aldous] Huxley feared was that there would be no reason to ban a book, for there would be no one who wanted to read one. Orwell feared those who would deprive us of information. Huxley feared those who would give us so much that we would be reduced to passivity and egoism. Orwell feared that the truth would be concealed from us. Huxley feared the truth would be drowned in a sea of irrelevance. Orwell feared we would become a captive culture. Huxley feared we would become a trivial culture, preoccupied with some equivalent of the feelies, the orgy porgy, and the centrifugal bumblepuppy."

These principles and sentiments were presaged in earlier American thought, as Thoreau wrote:

> "Our inventions are wont to be pretty toys, which distract our attention from serious things. They are but improved means to an unimproved end, an end which it was already but too easy to arrive at; as railroads lead to Boston or New York. We are in great haste to construct a magnetic telegraph from Maine to Texas; but Maine and Texas, it may be, have nothing important to communicate."[4]

Do not misunderstand: Within the sea of information we find knowledge and resources to empower today's producers; what we *do* with that increased power is the key. The role of producers in society is indispensable to freedom. Understanding the interplay of liberty and society through history can help us to expand the influence of entrepreneurs today.

Human Society Through The Ages

The great benefit of the Nomadic Age was family and community connectedness and a feeling of true belonging, while the Agrarian Age brought improved learning, science and art—and eventually, democratic freedoms. The Industrial Age allowed more widespread distribution of prosperity and social justice, and many improved lifestyle options through technological advances. Unfortunately, during the Industrial Age many freedoms were decreased as free nations turned to big institutions and secretive agencies for governance.

During the Industrial Age reliance on the conveyor belt model impacted nearly every major aspect of life—from education and health care to agriculture, industry, business, law, media, family, elder care, groceries, clothing, and on and on. Whether the end product was goods or services, these all became systemized on assembly lines—from production to delivery, and even post-purchase customer service.

At the same time, we widely adopted certain industrial views which became cultural, such as "Bigger is always better," "It's just business," "Perception is reality," among others. In practice, these maxims are quite often more false than true, but they nevertheless became the cultural norm.

Perhaps the most pervasive and insidious mantra promoted by modernism is that success in life is built on becoming an employee. Its academic corollary is that the purpose of education is to prepare for a job. Far too many adults tend to make their job-identity the focus and meaning of their adult life. And this allegiance does not adequately compensate them in terms of happiness, satisfaction or security.

By contrast, those with an entrepreneurial spirit who look on their professional pursuits as an expression of their purpose in life—harmonious with and complementary to their roles in family and community—not only have greater happiness, satisfaction and security, but also (through their producer mindset and entrepreneurial activities) leaven society and empower others to achieve a greater measure of these.

This is not to say that a person employed by someone else must therefore have an "employee mentality." The producer mindset is not the exclusive domain of owners and CEOs; certainly many producer-citizens are *intrapreneurs*—so-called "employees" within an organization who add much value to society and support freedom with their creativity, integrity and service ethic. The key to success in many profitable organizations turns on such individuals. A truly free and prosperous society is built on a system where a large number of the adult population spends its working days producing as owners, entrepreneurs, intrapreneurs and social leaders.

Producer *versus* Employee Society

A society of producers is more inclined to promote freedom than a society of dependents. Indeed, only a society of producers *can* maintain freedom. Most nations in history have suffered from a class system where the "haves" enjoyed more rights, opportunities and options than the "have nots." This has ever been a major threat to freedom.

The American framers overcame this by establishing a new system where every person was treated equally before the law. This led to nearly two centuries of gradually increasing freedom, opportunity and social progress.

During the Industrial Age this system changed in at least two important ways. First, the U.S. commercial code was changed to put constraints on investors and investment opportunities rather than simply offering legal remedies for *all* investors (rich or poor) as protection against criminal activity. In the name of protecting the "unsophisticated," laws were passed that allow only the highest level of the middle class and the upper classes to invest in the opportunities with the highest returns. In other words, investors were not only to be protected from criminals, but from themselves. So much for our celebrated American value of self-determination; so much for Adam Smith's "freedom to fail." This inequality before the law now created a European-style model where only the rich own the most profitable companies and get richer while the middle and lower classes are virtually stuck where they are.

The second Industrial Age "advancement" was that schools at all levels were reformed to emphasize job training rather than quality leadership education. Today great leadership education is still the fare at many elite private schools, but the middle and lower classes are expected to forego the "luxury" of opportunity-affording, deep leadership education and instead content themselves with the more "practical" and "relevant" one-size-fits-all job training. This significant change, though largely championed by well-intentioned and altruistic individuals, actually perpetuates the class system.

This is further exacerbated by the reality that public schools in middle class zip codes typically perform much higher than lower-class neighborhood schools. Private elite schools train most of our future upper class and leaders, middle class public schools train our managerial class and most professionals, and lower-class public schools train our hourly wageworkers. Notable and inspirational exceptions notwithstanding, the rule still is what it is.

Public policy reinforces the class system by the way the government runs public education, and the way big business self-perpetuates through the investment legal code. With these two biggest institutions in society promoting the class divide, lower and middle classes have limited power to change things.

The Power of Entrepreneurship

The wooden stake that overcomes the vampire of an inelastic class system is entrepreneurial success. Becoming a producer and successfully creating new value in society helps the entrepreneur surpass the current class-system matrix and also weakens the overall caste system itself. In short, if America is to turn the Information Age into an era of increased freedom and widespread economic opportunity, we need more entrepreneurs.

How do we accomplish this Freedom*Shift*? Well, first of all, we must lay aside the genie's lamp. We can polish it all day, but we might not be granted the wish that Congress simply change investment laws and allow everyone to be equal before the law. Neither government nor big business has a vested interest in this change, and neither, therefore, does either major political party. And all the idealistic rhetoric to the contrary, neither do incumbent legislators have a real vested interest in a much-needed overhaul of the educational system to emphasize entrepreneurial over employee training. Either of these wishes (or both) would be nice, but neither is likely.

What *is* more realistic is a grass-roots return to American initiative, innovation and independence. Specifically: Regular people of all classes need to become producers.

This is the crux of it all: A renaissance of entrepreneurship (building businesses), social entrepreneurship (building private service institutions like schools and hospitals), intrapreneurship (acting like an entrepreneur within an established company), and social leadership (taking entrepreneurial leadership into society and promoting the growth of freedom and prosperity) is needed.

Along with this, parents need to emphasize personalized, individualized educational options for their youth and to prepare them to be producers—whether as entrepreneurs or intrapreneurs—rather than cultivating in them dependence on employeeship.

If these two changes occur, we will see a significant increase in freedom and prosperity. The opposite is obviously true, as well: The long-anticipated "train wreck" in society and politics is not so difficult to imagine as it was twenty years ago. The education of the rising generation in self-determination, crisis management, human nature, history, and indeed, the liberal arts and social leadership in general, is the historically-proven best hope for our future liberty and success.

If entrepreneurial and other producer endeavors flourish and grow, their political clout will also grow, and it will naturally lead to changes in the commercial code that level the playing field for people from all economic levels and backgrounds. Until the producer class is growing, there is little incentive to deconstruct the class system. Over 80% of America's wealth comes from small businesses, and as these grow, so will our national prosperity.[5]

Today there are numerous obstacles to starting and growing small businesses. There will be many who justifiably mope that the current climate is not friendly to new enterprises. Frontiers have ever been thus, and our forebears plunged headlong into greater threats. What choice did they have? What choice do we have? What if they hadn't?

What if we don't?

The hard reality is that until producers are growing there will be little power to change this situation. As long as the huge majority is waiting for the government to provide more jobs, we will likely continue to see increased regulation on small business that decreases the number of new private-sector employment and opportunities. As Thomas L. Friedman wrote in *The New York Times*:

"[Says] Robert Litan, who directs research at the Kauffman Foundation, which specializes in promoting innovation in America: 'Between 1980 and 2005, virtually all net new jobs created in the U.S. were created by firms that were 5 years old or less....That is about 40 million jobs. That means the established firms created no net new jobs during that period.'

"Message: If we want to bring down unemployment in a sustainable way, neither rescuing General Motors nor funding more road construction will do it. We need to create a big bushel of new companies—fast....

"But you cannot say this often enough: Good-paying jobs don't come from bailouts. They come from start-ups. And where do start-ups come from? They come from smart, creative, inspired risk-takers."[6]

Entrepreneurs by nature aren't whiners, and they don't look for rescue outside of themselves. Because lawmakers have incentive to make law that benefits the majority of their constituents, and because the Employee Bloc *is* both vocal and self-interested, the voice of the entrepreneur won't be heard over the din of that majority—at least until there are more of them, and until they become more directly involved in the Great Conversation.

The only realistic solution is for Americans to engage their entrepreneurial initiative and build new value. This has always been the fundamental source of American prosperity. And government can help in a major way simply by getting rid of the many and growing regulations that hinder small businesses.

The Growing Popularity of Producer Education

Consider what leading books on the needs of American education and business are saying. Top futurist Alvin Toffler says in *Revolutionary Wealth* that schools must de-emphasize outdated industrial-style education with its reliance on rote memorization, the skill of fitting in with class-oriented standards, and "getting the right answers," and instead infuse schools with creativity, individualization, independent and original thinking skills, and entrepreneurial worldviews.

Harvard's Howard Gardner argued in *Five Minds* that all American students must learn the following entrepreneurial skills: "the ability to integrate ideas from different disciplines or spheres," and the "capacity to uncover and clarify new problems, questions and phenomena." Bestselling author John Naisbitt of *Megatrends* fame wrote in *Mindset* that success in the new economy will require the right leadership mindset much more than Industrial-Age credentials or status.

Tony Wagner wrote in *The Global Achievement Gap* that the skills needed for success in the new economy include such producer abilities as: critical thinking, problem solving, collaboration, leading by influence, agility, adaptability, curiosity, imagination, effective communication, initiative and entrepreneurialism.

Former Al Gore speechwriter Daniel Pink writes in *A Whole New Mind* that the most useful and marketable skills in the decades ahead will be the entrepreneurial abilities of high-concept thinking and high-touch leading. Seth Godin makes the same case for the growing need for entrepreneurial-style leaders in his business bestseller *Tribes*. Malcolm Gladwell arrives at similar conclusions in the bestselling book *Outliers*.

There are many more such offerings, all suggesting that the future of education needs to emphasize training the rising generations to think and act like entrepreneurs. Indeed, without a producer generation, the Information Age will not be a period of freedom or spreading prosperity. Still, few schools are heeding this research.

The response that we do see is largely cosmetic, as university websites and educational programs seem to say all the right things and employ the new buzz-words, but for the most part, still fail to fully implement meaningful changes. And how could they? Their tenured faculty are the designers of the programs and the authors of their texts. And with student finances and enrollment numbers all in question, they have bigger fish to fry; they hardly have the luxury of reinventing themselves when their institutional survival is on the line. Surely it must go without saying that if we are to see a resurgence of the producer mindset, we cannot rely upon academia to lead the charge.

CNN's Fareed Zakaria has shown in *The Post-American World* that numerous nations around the world are now drastically increasing their influence and national prosperity. All of them are doing it in a simple way, by incentivizing entrepreneurial behavior and a growing class of producers. Unlike aristocratic classes, successful entrepreneurs are mostly self-made (with the help of mentors and colleagues) and have a deep faith in free enterprise systems that allow opportunity to all people regardless of their background or starting level of wealth.

Entrepreneurs and Freedom

As more entrepreneurs succeed, the legal structure naturally becomes freer. As more people take charge of their own education, utilizing the experts as tutors and mentors but refusing to be dependent on the educational establishment, individualized education spreads and more leaders are prepared. With more leaders, more people succeed as producers, and the cycle fortifies and perpetuates itself.

Freedom is the result of initiative, ingenuity and tenacity in the producer class. These are also the natural consequences of personalized leadership education and successful entrepreneurial ventures. Our nation needs a rebirth of freedom—a Freedom*Shift*—and it must start with a grass-roots revolution of producer-citizens and social leaders.

History is full of anti-government fads, from the French and Russian revolutionists to tea party patriots in Boston and anti-establishment protestors at Woodstock, among many others. The revolutions that really last are led by tenacious entrepreneurial-thinking leaders who build businesses and organizations and thereby increase the prosperity and freedom of their society.

For anyone who cares about freedom and wants to pass the blessings of liberty on to our children and grandchildren, we need to get one thing very clear: A revolution of entrepreneurs is needed. We need more of them, and those who are already entrepreneurs need to become even better social leaders. Without such a revolution, freedom will be lost.

Five Types of Producers

Prosperity and abundance in a society depend on a certain type of person: the producer. Societies with few producers stagnate and decay, while nations with a large number of producers vibrantly grow—in wealth, freedom, power, influence and the pursuit of happiness.

Producers think in the language of abundance rather than scarcity, take initiative instead of waiting for someone else to provide them with opportunity, and boldly venture wise risks instead of surrendering to the fear that they can't make a difference.

In contrast, non-producers provide very little leadership in society and cause more than their share of the problems. Jefferson considered producers the most valuable of citizens. While he was thinking specifically of farmers, his extensive commentary on the subject illuminates his criteria for such praise of the georgics (workers of the land[7]), and the principles may be applied today to all those who add significant value to society. Non-producers consume the value that is added to society, but they create little value.

But who are the producers? Certainly Top 500 executives include themselves in this category; and so do small business owners in their first month of operation. Successful investors call themselves producers, as do unsuccessful day traders who claim that they just "haven't had their lucky break yet." Clearly, just calling yourself a producer doesn't make you one.

In fact, there are at least five types of producers, and each type is vital to a successful civilization. Each of the five creates incredible value, though the currency of the value is not always the same. Without producers of any of these types, no society succeeds and grows. With all five simultaneously creating sufficient value, no society has ever failed. Producers are vital—all five kinds of them.

1: Gurus

The highest level of value creation comes from prophets, sages and philosophers – which collectively, I label "Gurus." This category of producers is not limited to the Biblical-type prophets who spoke directly with God, but also includes thought-leaders who teach true principles. This makes gurus the most important of the producers, because without clearly understood principles all the other types of producers fail. Indeed, the other producers succeed precisely to the extent that they understand and apply true principles.

Guru-producers include Moses and Paul, who share God's wisdom with us, and also sages like Socrates or Confucius or Bastiat, thought leaders like Edward Deming or Peter Drucker, philosophers like Buckminster Fuller or Warren Buffet, and those who inspire us to serve like Billy Graham or Mother Teresa.

Whether you agree or disagree with these people, their lives and utterances invite you to think, ponder, consider, and ultimately understand truth. By applying these truths, a person is able to produce. Even if you just sit and ponder (letting the truths come to your mind through deep thought), or engage in deliberate effort toward a goal (learning through hard experience), true principles can still be passed to you through spiritual, intuitive or creative means.

God, or the Universe if you prefer, is the greatest producer of all, and He shares true principles with us so we can also produce. For value to be created, true principles must be applied. Ironically, because God, prophets, gurus and other wise people often share their wisdom without asking for monetary compensation, sometimes other types of producers misunderstand or underestimate their currency of exchange and discount the value of their contribution. But make no mistake: Revealing and teaching true principles is the highest level of creating value.

Whether we learn principles through inspiration or intuition, from the lessons gained through hard work and experience or from wise and caring mentors: Without principles we cannot produce. Parents and grandparents are among the most important producers, because they teach principles most effectively—or not. When they don't, the whole society suffers. When they do, the foundation for freedom, prosperity and happiness is firmly established.

2: Statesmen

The next type of value creation comes from statesmen. Statesmen are not to be confused with politicians and bureaucrats, who are often worse than non-producers because they actually both inhibit the creation of, and plunder, value. This is anti-producing and theirs is the currency of scarcity. In contrast, statesmen create freedom-value in society. The level of freedom in any nation is a direct result of the actions of statesmen—past and present.

If the contributions of great statesmen like Cato, Washington, Jefferson or Gandhi are present, a nation will throw off its enslaved past and adopt new forms and structures which ensure freedom of religion, freedom of choice and action, freedom of property and commerce, and other freedoms. With these freedoms aggregated, the value created can be called "life, liberty and the pursuit of happiness." Take these freedoms away, and entrepreneurship and investment will wane. There are no historical exceptions to this pattern.

Statesmen like Lincoln, Churchill or Margaret Thatcher keep a nation from rejecting its freedoms and moving back into a cycle of tyranny and anarchy, where little production of any kind of value can occur. In short, without principles there is little freedom, and without freedom all other kinds of production shut down, are regulated out of existence, and cease to be viable options. No matter how entrepreneurial your spirit, you would not have created much value in the economy of Nero's Rome, Russia under Stalin, or even Boston under the Stamp Act.

Without freedom, only gurus survive as producers (although even their survival often gets dicey)—all other types of producers need both principles *and* freedom to flourish. The greater the understanding of principles and the freedom of the society, the greater the opportunities for producers. Indeed, in the hierarchy of value, Freedom is second only to Truth.

Only when freedom is widespread would the other types of producers have the peace and luxury sufficient to believe that statesmen don't add value. And frankly, when the legacy of previously-won freedom is in its bloom – *that* is the very moment that it is in the greatest danger of being lost; for this is several generations after the statesmen have done their great work. At such times, it is critical that we see the rise of new generations of visionary Statesmen—individuals of character and competence, of virtue, wisdom, diplomacy and courage, who see clearly the dangers ahead and the solutions that their compatriots do not, and who fulfill their invaluable role in society as freedom producers.

Of course, the well-known statesmen like Lincoln or Jefferson only appear on the scene when there are a lot of lesser-known individuals studying, writing about, discussing and promoting statesmanship. History seems to indicate that for such world-moving luminaries to rise to prominence, there must be a fellowship of other like-minded individuals who contribute to the process within their circle of influence as they study, write, talk about and promote statesmanship. Generations with both the notable, iconic statesmen and the less-celebrated but equally important statesmen who are leaveners of society produce true freedom that allows widespread educational and economic opportunity.

Most of the history of the world is bereft of such statesman-ship, and as a result most of the people of the world were serfs, peasants, slaves and others who produced comparatively little and enjoyed even less. Yet I believe it is the true potential of all mankind to be producers, leaders, nobles. Jefferson called these the "natural aristocracy," and wholescale human progress of this kind only occurs during those rare stretches of history where statesmen create and perpetuate freedom. Next to principles taught by gurus, Freedom is the highest value that one can add to any society.

3 - 4: Investors and Entrepreneurs

The third type of producer is the Investor, and the fourth type is the Entrepreneur. These need little commentary among today's producers, who nearly all realize that entrepreneurship is neces-sary to create new economic value and that even the best entrepre-neurial ideas and leaders can fail without adequate capitalization.

More than a decade ago author Robert Kiyosaki listed Investors as the highest of his cashflow quadrants and Business owners, or entrepreneurs, next. He is right on. Without investors, many if not most entrepreneurs would fail. Entrepreneurs bring the ideas and the labor to the table, and the Investor commits the capital to empower the Entrepreneur. Without both Investors and Entre-preneurs, no society can make significant or sustained progress.

Moreover, without investment and entrepreneurship many of the principles taught by Gurus and most of the freedoms vouchsafed by Statesmen would never be fully experienced—and would eventually be lost. There is an interdependent dynamic between on the one hand, Gurus and Statesmen, and on the other hand, Investors and Entrepreneurs, because the Entrepreneur/Investor duo are the implementors of the ideas created and expanded by the Gurus and Statesmen. As previously stated, no society is re-ally successful unless all five types of producers effectively create value in their unique and interconnected ways.

Part of the value created by Investors and Entrepreneurs is obvious—they provide capital and establish institutions which build society. Virtually every family and individual benefits from their goods and services. Perhaps less known, but just as important: Investors add the essential value of experience. Buffet and nearly all successful investors affirm that without personal knowledge and significant experience in a Business, almost everyone who tries their hand at Investing fails. In this way, the Investor is often also a mentor to the Entrepreneur.

A society without adequate investment and entrepreneurship will see little, if any, progress.

An American, A Frenchman And A Russian

The old Cold War-era joke is told of an American, a Frenchman, and a Russian, lost in the wilderness, who find a lamp and rub it. Out comes a Genie. He offers them each one wish, for a total of three.

The American pictures the large ranch owned by the richest people in the valley where he grew up, and wishes for a ranch ten times its size (so that he can invest the surplus for even greater returns), with flowing streams and meadows full of horses and cattle. His wish is granted and he is transported home to his new life.

The Frenchman pictures the farm and cattle of the largest estate from his home province, and wishes for one just like it. Again, his wish is granted. Finally, the Russian pictures the land and herds of the rich family in the steppes where he grew up, and wishes that a drought kill the cattle, dry up the grass, and bankrupt the aristocratic family.

This play on stereotypes isn't really very funny (and frankly, in today's global economic climate the stereotypes need some retooling), though it brings big laughs with audiences of producers. They get it. The Frenchman in the joke, thinking like an entrepreneur, wants the good things that life provides, and is willing to go to work to produce them. The American, who thinks like an entrepreneur and an investor, is willing to go to work also, but wants to see his assets create more value.

The Frenchman wants value, the American plans for value, increased market share and perpetual growth. In contrast, the Russian in this parable can only think of one thing: getting even with those who seem to have more than him—not by being equally prosperous, but by tearing them down. This is the same as Steve Farber's lament about the sad state of our modern employee mentality—where "burn your boss" is a slogan of millions of workers who see "The Man" —their employer—as the enemy.

Don't bother asking what they'd do if the boss actually *did* run into trouble; they'd probably cough into their fists, mumble a change of subject and then scatter like roaches when the cellar light comes on—just before they lose their jobs to downsizing. Even Washington likes to join the blame game by pointing fingers at Wall Street, Main Street and everyone in business, generating programs and regulations that they have no idea how to fund, assuming that the brilliant and long-suffering entrepreneur can do their heavy lifting for them and put all to rights.

The Employee *versus* Owner Mindsets

Initiative, vision, effective planning, the wise use of risk, quality execution—all are the contributions of entrepreneurs and investors. Without them, any society will decline and fall. Yet the nonproducer mentality is often deeply ingrained in most people. For example, a visiting speaker at George Wythe University told the producer-minded student body of how challenging it was to get his employees out of their "employee" mentality.

As the founder of a growing manufacturing technology company, he pulled in all his two dozen employees and offered them liberal stock options. He explained that if the company met its projections, they would all be very wealthy—and he abundantly wanted to share the prosperity. Yet only a few of them would take the options. They only wanted cash salary, and mistrusted the whole concept of ownership.

When he first offered it, he assumed that they'd all jump on board. But when only a few did, he pulled them in one by one and tried to make the case for stock. Still, only a few more took the stock. The company grew, expanded, and then its value soared. Suddenly one month a half dozen of the company's employees were independently wealthy. They met and made plans; some stayed with the company and others moved on.

But the real story happened with the eighteen who had refused the stock. They were still paycheck-to-paycheck employees. And they were very angry! One by one they confronted the founder in his office, and many of the meetings ended with yelling, names called, and doors slammed. The entrepreneur couldn't believe it. *Now* these employees wanted *their* millions.

But it just doesn't work that way. "I *begged* you to take the stock," the owner told them. "Now, I can't help you. That stock now belongs to those who already bought in. Why didn't you take it when I offered?" he asked. They had no answer. Only: "I worked as hard as Jim and Lori, so why can't I get the same payment?"

Entrepreneurs and investors understand that work is very, very important, but that high levels of compensation come to those who create value and take calculated risk. This man's employees who chose the stock option were like the American in the joke above; they were choosing work combined with assets. The less "fortunate" employees felt ill-used, like the Russian in the joke. Consider the impact of this scarcity mentality on any society that adopts it. It bleeds into education, politics and all facets of life. Freedom is naturally lost, and prosperity slows down and eventually becomes poverty. Entrepreneurs and Investors are essential to societal success.

5: Intrapreneurs

The fifth type of producer is the Intrapreneur. In a free society, investment capital is plentiful—but only effective Entrepreneurs and Intrapreneurs can turn capital into increased value. This takes initiative, wise risk and leadership—just like the other types of producing.

While Entrepreneurs found or own businesses, Intrapreneurs work for and lead established businesses; but unlike traditional employees, Intrapreneurs work and lead with the Producer mindset. They run their department, team, or company with an abundance mentality, an attachment to true principles, and a fearless and informed faith in people and quality.

Intrapreneurs don't really have "jobs" even though they are often employees. Like Entrepreneurs, Intrapreneurs consider themselves on a mission to help society, to give it what it needs and wants, to truly serve others and improve themselves. Like all producers, they believe in a deep accountability, refuse to assign blame, don't believe in failure, and give their heart and soul to truly serve the customer and benefit society.

They add huge value in financial terms, in leadership, and in relationships—sometimes with people they've never met. They contribute quality in everything they do, and thereby deeply serve all who benefit from their product or service.

Great Entrepreneurs and Intrapreneurs have a deep faith in the market—as long as it doesn't go against true principles or subvert freedom. Without the initiative and risk of entrepreneurship, few Intrapreneurs would have a place to work and serve; likewise, without Intrapreneurs there would be few successful companies. Indeed, it is hard to imagine that there would be any.

The Synergy of Created Value

For any company to succeed, all five types of producers must fulfill their unique roles. This is even truer for any nation.

Producer	Currency
Guru	Principles
Statesman	Freedom
Investor	Capital
Entrepreneur	Prosperity
Intrapreneur	Quality

To see how vital all five types of producers are, consider the past. Major world powers in history have all declined and eventually failed in more or less the same way:

1. The people stop giving heed to the wisdom of the Gurus.

2. Voters (or those in power) replace Statesmen with politicians, whereupon freedom steadily decreases.

3. The natural result is increased regulations and taxation, frivolous lawsuits and judicial decrees, and governmental policies that discourage and then attack producers, initiative, and the abundance mentality in general.

4. Investment capital flees the nation to follow the Rule of Capital—it goes where it is treated well.

5. Finally, the people have a scarcity mentality, refuse to heed the Gurus or to empower Statesmen, Entrepreneurs leave to go where investment gives them opportunity and Intrapreneurs likewise lose their place. The nation stagnates and declines.

Egypt, Israel, Greece, Rome, Spain, Italy, Bismarck's Germany, and Han China all followed this pattern. Each was a major center of world power, influence and prosperity, and many declined into third-world nations. France copied this pattern in the 1800s; Britain followed it in the 1900s. The United States is on an identical track today.

Specifically, the U.S. is at the point where it is increasing its regulation, experiencing absurd lawsuits, court decisions and executive orders, and increasingly adopting policies that discourage investment and entrepreneurship. The next step is to openly attack investment and entrepreneurship, which is already occurring. And when investors find higher profits in other nations, while facing decreasing returns along with public hostility and rising taxes at home, U.S. investment dries up. The media style this as a credit shortage, but in reality the investment money is just being put to work in nations that treat capital better.

The only hope is for a new generation of producers to effectively promote freedom. In fact, the U.S. has been at this point before—once in 1860 and again in 1939. Both times enough statesmen—most of them forgotten by all except avid readers of history—arose to step up and save our freedoms.

Britain saw the same thing happen in 1216, 1620, 1815 and 1937. Other nations have followed a similar pattern. When the people listen to the Gurus, Statesmen promote freedom and Investors, Entrepreneurs and Intrapreneurs build the nation.

When the Gurus are ignored and statesmanship is seen as abstract and worthless, Investors go elsewhere—capital flees beyond the borders to other lands of opportunity, and the home country declines. Politicians blame big business and corporations blame government, while all along small business is undervalued and over-regulated—and government upsizing hurts the economy on many levels.[8] With such decline come moral decay, the loss of political and economic freedom, and the reduction of opportunity.

Abundance is a true principle; yet through history most governments have made it a major goal to curtail opportunity and channel prosperity to the aristocracy or royalty. Anyone who thinks this can't happen in America hasn't closely studied history.

Yet it doesn't have to be this way. No matter what government does, the producer spirit can flourish and bring a return to freedom and prosperity. It gets more difficult the longer entrepreneurship is disregarded; but as long as small business ventures are an option there is hope for freedom.

Those who are already successful or committed producers can help by avoiding the three predictable mistakes that producers often make. Anyone who knows these pitfalls and avoids them will be a better producer and create more lasting value in society.

Producer Mistake #1: The Generation Gap

First, producers too frequently discourage their own children from following the producer path. It is true that in their building years many young producers foreswear the life of unproductive privilege for their posterity, believing that they'll do all within their power to teach the abundance mindset to their children. And most of them do—until the children approach adulthood. At this point, many producers who are finally starting to enjoy some level of security and ease as a result of their labors seek now to help their children avoid the pain and sacrifice of this path.

Many producers encourage their children to become professionals—doctors, lawyers, accountants, engineers; they can afford to send them to such schools, so why not? It is ironic how many very successful college-dropout producers make sure that all of their children attend the most prestigious colleges available and major in the "normal" career fields. Many producers who succeed in spite of their conveyor-belt education rather than because of it make this mistake as well. They want to give their children the things they had to miss out on, and in the process, neglect to pass on to them the things they *did* have in abundance.

Even the producers who train their oldest child to follow in their path often send the younger children in other directions. And woefully few producers pass along the producer mindset to their grandchildren.

This is not intended to suggest that the family business must always stay in the family, or that the aspirations and affinities of our succeeding generations should be subordinated to the good of the company. But training our youth in social leadership, abundance, creating value, truly becoming your best, serving society and the producer mindset offers them an advantage no matter what path they take in life.

The historically effective solution for this is for producers to put real time, thought, planning and execution into their grandparenting role—even long before they are grandparents. Quality grandparenting is a way for all producers to engage the guru-prophet-sage-elder role for their family, and to help pass on their wisdom and understanding of true principles to future generations. Great parenting fulfills this same function, and is part of guruing—the highest level of production.

Producer Mistake #2: The Blinders

A second mistake many producers make is to think that their particular producer-role is the only one that creates *real* value. Like the old parable of the carpenter who believes that all of the world's ills can be fixed with a hammer, sometimes producers get so focused on their particular brand of producing that they dismiss the value of the others. Focus is good; but narrow thinking usually limits one's effectiveness.

For example, a Statesman who believes that changing government is the only real answer to society's ills and that freedom will fix all problems will likely reject the moral teachings of Gurus and consider them mere "philosophy." Such a person limits his statesmanship because he just doesn't get it.

Neither does the Statesman who thinks freedom is the only goal, and that Entrepreneurs are just in love with money; he will likely try to use law against entrepreneurship, which is the *opposite* of statesmanship. A true Statesman sees that all five types of producers are vital to society. Similarly, when Gurus, Sages and Prophets undervalue Statesmen, freedom of religion and independent thinking are often lost.

Likewise, an Entrepreneur who discounts the teachings of Gurus may feel successful because he's made a fortune selling filth and addiction. "After all, I just gave the market what it wanted," he says. "That makes me a selfless servant of the people." No abundance-minded entrepreneur would think this, because value is only created when principles of morality, freedom and personal dignity aren't attacked. If economic value reduces moral or freedom values, *absolute value* is actually decreased.

Or, consider the entrepreneur who thinks building profitable businesses is the only way to create value and therefore does little to promote statesmanship; in his older and wiser years he will likely regret the regulated and degenerating world that he sees his grandchildren inheriting.

When Entrepreneurs undervalue Statesmen, the politicians and bureaucrats win the day and capital is discouraged and eventually attacked. The wise Entrepreneur or Investor will see the great value added by Gurus and Statesmen, and he will create *more* value in his life because his broader view will help him make better and wiser decisions.

The examples could go on, but suffice it to say that significant problems occur when any of the five undervalues or even devalues any of the others. By contrast, when all five types of producers understand, highly value, and actively support each other, all types of producers experience synergy—and the value created is exponentially increased.

Producer Mistake #3: Arrogance

Finally, a third common mistake made by producers is to look down on non-producers. One of the true principles taught by Gurus and Prophets is that every person is inherently as valuable as any other. True abundance means that we respect the inherent value of each individual, whatever the chosen path, and we work to ensure that all people remain free to follow their conscience and live the life of their choosing.

Those who understand this point are the most effective producers, because they do it all for the right reasons—a true love of self and desire to serve others. This is what abundance really means. Everything else falls short. This is true abundance—so abundant that you spend your life voluntarily improving yourself and serving others. (In contrast, true scarcity would be to spend your life on yourself.) Real value means *people value*—and creating value really means *helping people choose better lives*. This is what all five types of producing are all about.

Producer Families

If a revolution of new producers is to occur, there must be a renaissance of the family. Whatever happens in Washington, Wall Street, Main Street, Hollywood or Silicon Valley in the next ten years, it will all be irrelevant if our families don't come together at a much higher level. Without a renaissance of family, no new candidate can rise to save us. No new legislation, policy or program will heal our land.

On the other hand, the buttressing and revitalization of our society at the most basic level of family, though it be quiet and virtually ignored, is the most powerful catalyst to the revitalization of our freedom and prosperity. As families understand freedom and prosperity, they will help young people honor and value producers and find producer mentors. As long as nearly all families believe the doctrine of "Success in Life is a Good Job," it will be difficult for enough young people to break the mold and engage entrepreneurial and other producer lifestyles.

Parents are a vital type of producer that encompass the principles, forms, mindset, risks and values of all the rest. Indeed, they are the first and most formative gurus, statesmen, investors, entrepreneurs and intrapreneurs for most children and youth.

The Renaissance of Family

In crisis periods of history like the one we are now experiencing (as we shift from Industrial to Information society), almost everything changes. Economies change, as do governments, businesses, schools and cultures—often in dramatic and surprising ways.

Since few of us want to admit that the cycles of history[9] are driving things, most people are frustrated and feel vulnerable and even victimized by the widespread changes. Many turn to government to solve our most pressing problems, hoping it can work miracles. Sometimes it almost can; other times it falls tragically short.

Many turn to other institutions, or their own efforts, for solutions. Too few realize, however, the power of families in such times. Indeed, increased financial challenges and difficult world events often amplify the pressure on marriage and family relationships. Divorce rates increase, family dysfunction grows, and people look outside the family for more and more help—at the very time family members need each other and can help each other the most. This means that pressure on families is almost certain to increase for the years ahead.

As the Family Goes, So Goes the Nation

Shifting Periods (or "Crisis" Periods) in history are preceded by Good-Times Periods and then followed by Rebuilding Periods. If the cycles of history hold true and we face major challenges in the decades ahead, families will need even more internal strength.

I am an optimist, and I'm convinced that great things are ahead for America and the world. At the same time, I'm pretty clear about one thing: Our nation and our world will rise no higher than our families. If the family continues to decline, so will peace, prosperity, freedom and happiness.

Experts may cite studies and graphs outlining the details, but history is absolutely clear on this point: *The future of the family is the future of our world;* and whether yours is traditional or non-traditional, single parent, mentor/guardian, grandparent-as-parent, or sibling raising siblings, etc., you are included in this great opportunity.

A Disturbing Divergence From the Past

In past Crisis Periods, layoffs and failed businesses have resulted in the family pulling together—planting gardens, starting businesses, chopping wood to save on fuel and otherwise facing and working to overcome challenges together. In our current world, with its urbanized and technologically advanced lifestyle, we don't seem to be following this pattern of family retrenchment at the same pace or level as in the past.

We aren't relying less on paychecks and more on the family farm, or even leaving the family farm to find opportunity in places like the New World (1780s), the West (1860s), or California (1930s). In our time, no geographical Promised Land has arisen to deliver us.

At the same time, the modern world keeps us busy and separated from each other—kids at school, youth with groups of friends, mom and dad holding down multiple jobs or seeking employment, etc. Even where both adults in some homes are unemployed, they often don't spend more time together, but rather cope with their stresses and seek solutions independently. One of the great benefits of producer culture is the higher rate of time spent with family on shared goals.

For many people, diminished finances for vacations, no time off at a new job, productivity-related compensation and workplace competitiveness all bring pressure to de-emphasize family time and increase work time. The technologies that used to be tools to help connect us have turned on their masters. No longer luxuries, they have gone from being pervasive to invasive to divisive; each family member has his own unique and virtual social life, and family life sometimes suffers as a result.

We have sacrificed the needs of the family to those of the corporation for over five decades, and the results are starting to become painful.

The average American couple in 2009 spent only 16 minutes a day talking with each other, according to a report in *Men's Health*. Half of that time was spent discussing things like household chores and finances, leaving very little time to build relationships. The same *Men's Health* reported that "lack of quality time" was the number one cause of tension in couples' relationships—more than finances, work issues or other challenges.

Though the historical catalysts for family togetherness are all around us, we are actually spending *less* time together just talking and having fun as couples and families. Rather than refocusing on our marriages and family relationships, we are too often pulling even further apart.

The Potential Tragedy of Lost Opportunities

The simplistic reason that Good-Time Periods turn into Crisis Periods is that families turn away from each other to serve the agendas of corporations, marketing firms, schools and others. Crisis Periods are all about recapturing the most important things—especially happy and successful families. If families don't come together, strengthen communities, build new entrepreneurial enterprises and begin to rebuild society, we won't see the benefits of a great Rebuilding Period ahead.

This is a potential tragedy of Dark Ages proportions. Just consider Rome in the first century, France in the late Seventeenth Century, the South after the Civil War, or modern Cambodia, Bosnia or Rwanda. A society has no destiny that is not tied to the strength of its families. Without a family renaissance, *no* society rebounds from crisis. And family renewal is led by parents who think like leaders and producers in the home.

The Good News

The good news in all this is that the bad news **IS** good news: If the biggest challenge in our families is lack of quality time and taking the time to really talk, then the solutions are simple. What if you spent less time correlating with your spouse about things that seem urgent, and a lot more time with your spouse talking about *less urgent* and *more important* things—even doing more "fun" things and simply enjoying each other? What if you did the same with each of your children, siblings and/or parents? Not everyone has all these options, but clearly not enough of those who do have families are giving them the needed attention and effort. It's trite but true that if it all comes crashing down, we will hardly regret having invested more in our families.

The currency of family producers is Love, and it is the gold that backs all the currencies created by the other 5 types of producers.

What if families spent two or three evenings a week and a day each weekend doing fun things, entrepreneurial ventures and/or service projects together? *Together* is the key word here. This is truly the way that major challenges in history are solved at the grass roots. When families find their default setting is spending time together—even doing not-much-of-anything—their interactions take place in what I like to call "the right kind of vacuum"; in that space, ideas and solutions (whether personal or societal) are generated at a family level.

Of course, this only works where families both bond within and connect without—not isolating themselves, but strengthening their relationships with each other and the rest of their community. And it works most effectively where families resist the temptation to draw factional "us/them" lines and instead reach out and build relationships on newly-found common ground, as people of all stripes and creeds seek to compensate for the loss of forms, ideas and institutions that no longer promise security and providence. An across the board getting-back-to-basics mentality reveals that on a fundamental level, we have much more in common than had been apparent in a different time and climate. As families respond to the challenges in our world by investing in the Core unit of society, individual happiness, family unity, community strength, and national security and prosperity will all be impacted for the better.

The Little Things That Make A Huge Difference

Here is the pattern: improve marriages, strengthen family relationships, make new friends, and build stronger connections with friends and community. These are producer roles, applied in the most important of all organizations: the family. This naturally overcomes Crisis; and without it, Crisis Periods worsen and persist.

Again: Whatever happens in Washington, Wall Street, Main Street, Hollywood or Silicon Valley in the next ten years, it will all be irrelevant if our families don't come together at a much higher level. Ironically, it is the little things that will most likely win (or lose) this battle for the future of freedom and prosperity.

In the next decade, improving your marriage one hour a day (at least) may be the most important thing you can do for society. Same with many hours a week spent actively talking with and doing activities together with children and grandchildren. Seldom has so much depended on such little things!

Will we follow the course of societies past that have lost their way and crumbled under the devastating forces of economic upheaval, war and other crises? Or will we pull together as families and communities to create a brighter future? If we get it right, we will also see a renaissance of nations. No matter what experts may say or what historians may someday write about our times, it will certainly be defined by either the Decline or the Renaissance of the Family.

How to Become a Producer

Producers are the most important citizens, as Thomas Jefferson put it. Actually, the word he used was farmers—specifically, "tillers of the soil." By producing food, farmers obviously had an important role in successful society. But Jefferson meant more than this. Because farmers lived close to the land they were self-reliant with respect to their own survival and received an income from providing indispensable basic needs for others. This made them more independent than people of other occupations. If hard times came, they tightened their belts and lived off their farms. In contrast, during the same challenges, most city dwellers and even shop owners were more likely to turn to the government or upper classes for help.

The founding generation was critical of the level of dependency among the European populace. The small but incredibly powerful upper class was the only group that could live off their assets and make it through hard times like war, economic depression or pandemic. Because of this, the upper class was independent while everyone else was dependent on the upper classes and government.

Since the first focus of human societies is to survive, the power to survive independently was seen as true independence. Indeed, the War of Independence had this deeper meaning to founding Americans: They were finally independent of the European upper class.

Dependents *versus* Independents

In our day, a vast majority of people is dependent either on an employer or the government—or both. One way to rate your level of independence might be to measure how long you can survive, feed your family and live in your home after your employer stops paying you anything. Some people are two-year independents, while others are three-year independents or two-month independents, and so on. It is not unlikely that most Americans are absolute dependents, living paycheck to paycheck or on government support.

The triple entendre here is interesting. At a time where (1) the growth of *political independents* is helping lessen the dangers of a two-party monopoly on American politics, there is a need for more people to become (2) true *economic independents* (people who can survive indefinitely without a paycheck). As both of these grow, (3) the level of American *independence* will increase.

Any level of economic independence is good, including everything from two months to twenty years of non-employer-dependent financial security. But the future of freedom may well depend on those with permanent economic independence.

Three Types of Independents

There are three groups with long-term independence, three groups whose members are more or less permanently free from dependence on a paycheck. The first two are made up of people supported by trust funds or equivalent, covered financially for life by wealth earned or passed down to them.

Group one lives off these funds, often spending their lives in play and leisure. The second group uses their trust funds or wealth to spend their lives dedicated to making a difference in society, through service, career, investment, entrepreneurship, philanthropy or whatever path they choose to use to improve themselves and the world.

The third group has no trust fund or equivalent wealth to rely upon, but has the skill set and worldview of entrepreneurial enterprise. This group doesn't start with full bank accounts, but rather with rich personal resources consisting of faith and determination, grit and initiative, and an undying belief in the principles of abundance, hard work and enterprise.

Whatever happens, members of this third group have an almost unshakable belief that there is opportunity everywhere. They believe in themselves, and have the conviction that if they put their minds and hands to work they can build value out of opportunity and create prosperity through their energy and effort.

Together, the second and third groups are society's Producers—its Social Leaders. They start, build, invest in, work in and grow businesses and organizations that create a nation's assets, advancements and top achievements. They employ the workers of the world. And when hard times come, they don't ask government or employers to provide for them; rather, they look around, assess the situation, see opportunities amidst the problems, and get to work building value for the future.

They do, however, implore government and the big established businesses to get out of the way, to allow them the freedom to turn their initiative and work into growing profits and success. When government increases obstacles and regulations on small business, it directly attacks freedom and prosperity. When this occurs, entrepreneurs naturally look for nations and markets that are friendly to business. As a result, nations with free enterprise systems attract more producers and are blessed with greater wealth and prosperity.

Non-Producer Attempts to Create Producers

Nations naturally benefit from a large producer class, but how are producers created? The common answers fall short.

The liberal view is that those with credentials and advanced education, the experts, must set up a system that allows enterprise but also fairly distributes the rewards of economic success. The conservative view is to allow big investors to get huge rewards and therefore be willing to take big risks. The blue-collar populist approach is to make sure management treats labor fairly and humanely. The bureaucratic view is that rules make the society and economy work.

While each of these has a place in the balance, none of them really get to the heart of what makes producers tick. The problem is that these views are nearly always promoted and managed by employees with an employee background and an employee mentality. Non-producers grudgingly (or philosophically) admit the great need for more producers, and then set out to build conveyor belts that will produce more producers. This sometimes works inadvertently—insofar as a non-conforming cog sometimes locates his or her producer mojo in the process of overcoming the obstacles afforded by the conveyor-belt system and breaks free to find entrepreneurial success.

David Brooks has referred to Washington's party politics as the PhDs (liberals) *versus* the MBAs (conservatives). Both give lip service to small business; but their modus operandi belies a different governing worldview.

The PhDs want government to run the economy and provide jobs, and to be the Great State Entrepreneur so that regular citizens don't need to take risks. The MBAs want to appeal to big investment, and are loathe to consider small business significant or meaningful. Both are prompt to fund programs and projects with the revenues largely generated by the operations of small businesses, while shoveling equal parts of regulation and contempt upon them. The average citizen-employee either wants to "stick it to the man" or just wants managers to treat employees better. To sum up: All of these, from the PhDs and MBAs down to the mailroom, are frequently guilty of employee-mentality thinking.

Government programs will not create many entrepreneurs, nor will most corporate ventures, bureaucratic agencies or labor unions. And most MBA programs emphasize employee training and measure their effectiveness by citing job placement statistics. Entrepreneurs are the natural competitors to all these.

The Answer

How do we create more producers? The answer, as frustrating as it is to the experts, is:

We don't.

That is, institutionalized and standardized programs do not of themselves yield producers, except by happenstance (as noted above). Not to put too fine a point on it, but: The very act of systemizing the training of initiative and innovation tends to *shut down initiative and innovation.*

What *can* be done, what actually *works*, is to help young people realize the importance of producers in society and reward their inclinations toward being anomalies, outliers and disruptive innovators. The first one is easier said than done; the second one is nearly impossible for most parents and teachers to either conceive of or to value, much less to accomplish.

To support the development of the entrepreneurial spirit in the rising generation, youth need to be:

1. Exposed to those who highly value entrepreneurialism

2. Given opportunities to earn and receive personalized mentoring from successful producers

In short, as we elevate the honor and accessibility of being producers, we will tend to increase the number of them.

It is interesting to study the most successful network marketing, multi-level and other like organizations that in recent times have emphasized entrepreneurship among "regular" people.

Top brands in network marketing and their affiliates have created more millionaires than the top 100 corporations, with each millionaire being an independent entrepreneur. In such organizations, interested people are introduced to many who highly value entrepreneurial producers, and new affiliates work directly with a producer mentor. Network marketing is a proven tool for leadership development, and many networking companies have state-of-the-art systems to develop leadership; and they are led by field leaders—not the companies themselves.

Hundreds of non-traditional companies have accomplished these types of results. Ironically, one criticism of such organizations by mainstream (employee) experts is that they are pyramid schemes. From another perspective, it could be said that the true pyramid companies are those where most of the work hours are done by lesser-paid employees while the highest salaries and bonuses go to the executives at the top.

Hands-on business schools like Acton MBA and Rand have similarly helped educate entrepreneurs using a combination of inspiring people to be producers and also providing producer mentors. And the many bestselling books promoting this same model, from the "One Minute" series to the writings of Steve Farber, Jim Ferrell and many others, show that this system is resonating with many people and starting to gain some traction.

Highly successful coaching services have followed this pattern as well, including such notable businesses as those established by John Assaraf, Leslie Householder, Dennis Deaton and many of those mentioned in *The Secret*. Nearly the entire self-help industry is built on this model: Promote the honor and value of successful entrepreneurialism and help would-be producers get direct mentoring from successful producers. Thinkers like Andrew Carnegie and writers like Dale Carnegie outlined this model a long time ago.

The mainstream PhD/MBA ambivalence toward the "Success" and "Self-Help" community stems from their reliance on and loyalty to the doctrine of employeeship. Harvard Business School has noted that the major changes in the world tend to come from what have been called "disruptive innovators."[10] These anomalous individuals produce surprising novelties from out-of-the-mainstream sources and dramatically change society, business, and other facets of life. Disruptive innovators are disruptive *precisely because* they are totally unexpected by the conventional majority and experts.

The government and big corporations spend a lot of resources trying to predict and anticipate the future. And invariably entrepreneurial producers come along every few years and change everything. Reams of articles and books are written trying to predict where the next such innovations will come from and prescribing how to help train future innovators. But the multi-level and other non-traditional entities drastically out-produce government and big corporate attempts to build entrepreneurs.

To summarize: We cannot institutionalize non-institutional results.

The Real Point

But all of this commentary still falls short of the real point. Only the *individual* can truly become an entrepreneur. If there is to be a much-needed revolution that brings many more entrepreneurs to society, individuals and families must take action and lead out. If what we want is more *independence*, then we must have more *independents*—more producers. If you want society to be leavened by a greater proportion of individuals with producer mojo, then you need to consider whether you should be a producer yourself, and how to become one. To be a producer, it is up to you to make it happen. Here are some suggestions:

First, study successful producers.

The most important part of this is to see the power of focus, integrity and faith in abundance that producers exemplify. Whereas the media often tries to paint producers as greedy and immoral, the truth is often very different. Pay special attention to what great producers believe, and learn to think like them. The habit of truly believing in abundance and principles makes one a true independent, permanently free of dependence on others and able to build, create and lead.

Second, study what the great producers study.[11]

The material most studied by the greatest producers and leaders has been the great classics. But producers are voracious readers, going far beyond any prescribed lists. Leaders are readers. Read the greatest works of mankind and everything else you can get your hands on. Keep reading, studying and learning throughout your life.

Third, find and work with mentors who are successful producers.

The unwritten lessons gained from this kind of experience are invaluable, real and profound. Coming face-to-face with greatness by working with successful producers is essential to becoming a successful producer yourself.

Finally: Get Off the Conveyor Belt.

Why is more entrepreneurial, innovative and leadership education flourishing in small, humble, usually under-funded environments than in the prestigious, elite halls of endowment and status? And even when the mainstream and elite institutions take note and attempt to emulate such successes, why do they fall short of the smaller talent hotbeds?

The answer is simple. The breeding grounds of initiative and leadership implement the philosophy of individualized education. This helps explain why so many disruptive innovations are initiated and led by "outliers,"[12] what Daniel Coyle called "chicken-wire Harvards". Indeed, Harvard, Yale, Stanford and their counterparts may lead the analysis about innovations, but "chicken-wire Harvards" produce so many more innovative projects.[13]

Nearly everywhere else, the emphasis is on systemized models of learning that students must learn to navigate and conform to. To reinforce this point by contrast: there are many small, humble and under-funded educational models that are *not* talent hotbeds; invariably they are followers of the conveyor-belt model rather than individualization.

Dead Poet's Society

I well remember a visit years ago to a private school that had just received two major breakthroughs: an endowment from a wealthy parent, and a new president who promised to significantly grow the school.

As I talked to this president, however, I realized that he fully intended to turn this excellent, proven hotbed of talent into a systemized conveyor belt. He felt that this is what the wealthy donor wanted—and maybe it was. But I could tell after a few minutes of visiting with him that the depth, quality and excellent results the school had boasted for the past decade would soon become little more than memories from the school's glorious past.

Five years later, my worst fears for this sweet little academy were unfortunately the reality. The school was no longer a place of deep quality and excellence, but it was much bigger, more bureaucratic, and hardly distinguishable from the local compulsory schools. Indeed, several charter schools in the area offered much higher quality.

The key to this change was teachers. In the public schools, teachers have been penalized for great teaching since 2002. As Harper's noted:

> "Under the No Child Left Behind Act of 2002...U.S. teachers are forced to choose between teaching general knowledge and 'teaching to the test.' The best teachers are thereby often disenfranchised by the improper use of education information systems."[14]

In most private schools, this system is not mandated. However, when such schools apply the systems approach to education, they usually obtain similar mediocre results.

In the old, underfunded days of the high school in our example, the teachers had given their hearts and souls to provide personalized, individualized attention to every student. As the school turned to industrial systems, these teachers were forced to move on or change their approach from individualized learning to factory-style academia.

Approaching each child with the assumption that she has genius inside, and that the teacher's role is to help her find it, develop and polish it to improve herself and the world—this is called teaching. Where it occurs, excellence flourishes. Anything else is something else.

This is applicable at all levels, from elementary to high school, undergraduate to graduate, and also adult learning. Individualization of education is the first step to leadership education, and without it quality is always decreased.

The Chemistry of Genius?

Science is now beginning to show the reasons why quality in education increases with individualization. Studies have shown what parents and teachers already know: that students receiving personalized, caring and quality mentorship learn more effectively than those required to conform to a deeply structured and systemized model. Elites have historically been successful in engaging tutors, mentors and individualizing private schools over less personal conveyor-belt schooling options.

Scientists are now discovering that the individualized method (personalized mentoring, deep practice, long hours of inspired, intrinsically-motivated and enthusiastic academic effort) results in drastically higher levels of the neural insulator myelin than the standardized system of education.[15]

Students with higher levels of myelin learn more and remember it longer. It is especially valuable for gaining, maintaining and polishing skills.

This research is in its infancy, but it is extremely suggestive that there may be neurochemical factors in our basic psychophysiology that are impacted by our learning environment. Maria Montessori, Charlotte Mason and other great educators hinted at this long ago, and there are chicken-wire Harvards across the globe that are following their lead. Personalized educational models, with dedicated and caring mentors helping learners achieve depth and inspiration in their studies, achieve better results than assembly-line education.

Mentoring Matters

Quality mentors help students learn at least three key things:

1. how to see their internal greatness and potential

2. how to study and practice in ways that greatly increase the flow of learning

3. how to repeat this kind of learning environment at will

These are nearly always individualized lessons.

To increase learning success (i.e. increase myelin levels) and create talent hotbeds, Coyle says, mentors must create an environment of individualized coaching, be perceptive in seeing individual needs in their students, use shock or passion or intensity to open student minds and then share valuable information, and find ways to really connect with each learner. All of this is traditional leadership education, based on the same principles as the 7 Keys of Great Teaching[16] covered in my book *A Thomas Jefferson Education*:

1. Classics, not Textbooks

2. Mentors, not Professors

3. Inspire, not Require

4. Structure Time, not Content

5. Quality, not Conformity

6. Simplicity, not Complexity

7. You, not Them (lead out by example)

Individualization Breeds Innovation

One thing is clear, if not yet conclusively established by science: Most parents and teachers who apply the 7 Keys see significant, drastic and lasting increases in the quality of their students' and their own learning. Personalized education is more effective in helping students learn in their areas of interest; but it also outperforms generally, as well as in math, science and technology.

In the decades ahead, as in decades past, many of the most innovative ideas and projects are likely to come from talent hothouses outside the mainstream, places where dedicated and caring mentors help young people see their huge potential, start to discover their great inner genius, and feel inspired to do the hard and effective work of getting a great education. Individualized, mentored, intensive learning has better results than standardized, rote and minimum-standards systems.

In addition to schools, this is taking place in non-traditional business models and wherever great mentors help would-be producers follow their dreams. Brady and Woodward's book *Launching a Leadership Revolution* is a great resource for doing just this.

Our society desperately needs more producers. We need more people who think like entrepreneurs and more people who take initiative and fulfill the needs of society without waiting for government or the people of wealth and privilege to "fix it for us." The future of freedom is directly and literally tied to the future of producers in our society.

Hamilton v. Jefferson

Thomas Jefferson envisioned a nation of small farm and shop owners that spread around leadership and prosperity, while Alexander Hamilton preferred a mercantile system with a few wealthy owners employing the large majority of the populace. Hamilton felt that an increase in wealth among the leading families would make up for the reduced freedom and less-widespread prosperity under a mercantile economy—after all, this was the model used by the most prosperous and powerful nations in Europe.

After the Great Depression, America decided to follow Alexander Hamilton's model instead of the Jeffersonian system, and a number of changes occurred which now haunt our generation. We have now reached a point where the greatest challenges we face are *caused* by the mercantile system and can likely only be solved by an entrepreneurial mindset.

Failed Solutions

Unfortunately, in the current political debate the two sides emphasize government solutions (more government-provided jobs and stricter regulation against corporations and bonuses) *versus* big-business mercantilism (hire and fire as best fits company projections, and move operations abroad to less hostile regulatory environments with cheaper labor—or in other words, business as usual). A third view comes from frustrated populists who want Washington to get its act together and fix the economy.

All three of these views miss the point. Wall Street, Washington and Main Street still seek Hamiltonian solutions: "Big institutions should fix things for us." The specific challenges we face, however, don't lend themselves to institutional fixes. Our current problems need precisely entrepreneurial-type solutions. This isn't the old debate of whether public or private programs are best. The truth is, that debate nearly always promoted institutional fixes. What we need now are patently non-institutional innovations.

Major Challenges

Consider the major problems we are facing. Most are the natural results of too much reliance on institutional size and power and not enough initiative, innovation and leadership from "little guys." Of course, the few who are entrepreneurs do an amazing job against increasing odds. But a major shift to the Entrepreneurial Mindset is needed to overcome our current challenges; and more such challenges will continue to arise as long as we struggle with our addiction to big institutions.

Specifically, the major concerns we're facing in the years and decades ahead include the following:

- Running out of money for social security and many other entitlements

- The flight of many in the entrepreneurial class to Brazil, India and other places with less regulation of small business

- The wartime economy of China that is built to thrive in times of conflict

- The end of privacy as government is pressured to oversee all people and things in the name of security and protection from terrorism

- The end of America's production base as industry continues to go abroad—and we continue to train the world's attorneys instead of more engineers and inventors

- The growing gap between rich and poor in the U.S. and globally

Also consider the following items that will peak and commence declining in the years immediately ahead, as outlined in the book *Peak Everything* by energy expert Richard Heinburg:

- Oil availability and cheap fossil fuels to drive the economy
- Fresh water availability per capita
- Easy, cheap, quick mobility
- Available land in agricultural production
- Political stability
- Safe, inexpensive food

Only one of these looming challenges (security against possible Chinese aggression) can be reasonably confronted directly by government, as it is now constituted. And even this could be beyond the government's scope if attacks are not military but cyber war on, say, America's financial records or utility providers.[17] A truly free government emphasizing a free enterprise economy would help against all of these, by empowering entrepreneurial action, wealth and innovation to meet each challenge.

Heinburg's solution to these problems is "fifty million farmers," which he describes as a drastic increase in the number of small farmers. Such people, Jefferson predicted long ago, own their own land and bring initiative and tenacity to producing food—and free citizens.

While the problems we face are clearly greater than a mere shift to locavorism will remedy, reviving the heart and mind of the citizen farmer is a good start. In addition to farmers, we need millions of producers of all kinds applying entrepreneurial talents and skills to overcoming our biggest challenges.

Habits and Complexes

There are at least two major roadblocks hindering this needed Freedom*Shift*. The first is habit. Our society has become habituated, at times addicted, to certain lifestyles. For example, when recession hit in 2008-2009, people spent more money, not less, at McDonald's. We are habituated to eating out, and tightening our belts in hard times has come to include eating even more french fries.

Perhaps our most debilitating rut as a culture is a dependence on experts. Until we kick this dependency, how can we rise above the statistics and become a nation of entrepreneurs and leaders? The answer, as challenging as it is, is for entrepreneurs to show us the way, and to keep at it until more of us start to heed.

The second huge roadblock is our complexity. Indeed, we have reached a level of complexity where simplicity itself is suspect. For example, the simple reality is that jobs migrate to less difficult nations. It's the old Rule of Capital: Capital goes where it is treated well. In nations that have become too complex, taxes and regulation cause at least a doubling of the amount employers must spend on labor. Many experts call this "progress," but the natural result is that many companies respond by sending their operations and jobs to less costly nations.

When this happens, complex nations react in an amazing way: They villainize the companies ("greedy profiteers") rather than reducing taxes and regulations to entice companies back home. Then they take an incredible extra step: They increase taxes and regulations even more on the businesses that stayed! What is the result? More money flees and recession inevitably comes.

At this point, when the need is obviously to lure businesses, capital and jobs back home with decreased regulation and taxes, nations that are too complex actually compound the negative situation as angry workers cry out for more regulations and controls. Freedom, prosperity and stability all suffer.

People who point out how ridiculous this is are often labeled extremists or radicals. Simple answers aren't often very popular in complex nations. Sadly, it usually takes a major crisis to get people to consider simple solutions.

Poor Complexion

Another example is found in the issue of health care. Health care costs consistently increase where voluminous regulations along with medical lawsuits lead to burgeoning malpractice insurance costs. When government seeks to regulate and force the costs down, it must find a way to reduce litigation and payouts.

But in complex society, people want to have their cake and eat it too. They want health care to cost less and also to leave doctors and insurance companies paying for incredibly expensive lawsuits. *How is it possible to get both?* "The government should make it so," is the answer of a complex society. *But how?* "The government should just fix it."

This amazingly naïve view of things is the result of complexity. Far too many citizens don't even expect to be able to understand the issue, so they leave it to the "experts." And once all is in the hands of experts, they are expected to solve everything without any pain or problem to the populace. After all, they're the experts, right?

Those who benefit most from the costs of lower health care either need to forego the threat of so many lawsuits or be willing to pay higher prices. But such simple answers don't convince in complex societies.

One more example is interesting. Hamilton argued in *The Federalist Papers* that for society to be free the legal code would need to be long, detailed and difficult to understand. He based this on the systems in Europe at the time. But ironically, these were the very systems the founders fought to abandon.

In contrast, Jefferson, Madison and many others taught that complex laws and legal codes were sure signs of oppression. They agreed with Montesquieu, Locke and Hume that laws must be simple, concise and brief, and indeed that the entire legal code must be simple enough that every citizen knows the entire law. If a person doesn't know the law, they argued, he shouldn't be held accountable for breaking it—or freedom is greatly reduced.

In complex society, by contrast, not only does the average voter not know the whole law, but neither do the law enforcement, the jurors, the legislators, or even the attorneys.

The Right Level of Complexity

The main criticism of simple societies is that they can tend to be intolerant, controlling and narrow-minded. This is an accurate and fair criticism, and such simple societies are not the ideal. Indeed, Madison shows the negatives of such societies in Federalist 18 through 20. He proposes that by establishing a large nation and a free constitution we can simultaneously establish both an open, modern and progressive society and a free, prosperous and happy nation.

Fortunately, we are not forced to choose between a narrowly simple nation and an overly complex one. The ideal is a nation sufficiently complex to promote progress, toleration, cooperation and growth and one with enough simple common sense to achieve freedom, prosperity and opportunity. This is the traditional entrepreneurial mix.

Whereas mercantilism values a few cosmopolitan elites employing a population of less urbane managers and workers, in contrast the entrepreneurial challenge has always been to balance complex and intricate details with simple and effective systems and results. In short, we need more entrepreneurs running more small, medium and large institutions in society. It is unfortunate we are trending toward less and less of our leaders having private-sector leadership experience.

Lifestyles of the Rich and Famous

The success of the next few decades will depend on certain types of people with certain skills and abilities. The talents and habits of "The Company Man" came into vogue in the 1950s and helped create a society of professionals, experts and officials. This greatly benefited the final decades (1955-2000) of the Industrial-Age surge.

But as the Information Age moved past infancy (1964-1991) and began its rebellious growth to adulthood (1992-2008), many became aware that change was ahead. As the Information Age grasps maturity and takes over in the 2010s and 2020s, major alterations in society are inevitable.

The Company Man is now replaced by what David Brooks called Patio Man[18]: Individualists who want personal freedom, enough income to pay the bills plus some extra spending money, a government that provides national security and keeps jobs plentiful, a nice house, a nice car each for him and her, a grill, a good movie tonight and friends over for the big game on Sunday. At first this was paid for by one working parent, then by both. But unless something changes, this lifestyle is at an end for all but the wealthiest tenth of the population.

The thing that facilitated such a lifestyle in the first place was the prosperity generated by entrepreneurship, and the only thing that can maintain such a lifestyle and still pay off our society's debts and obligations is a drastic increase in the number of entrepreneurs. Period.

Specific Entrepreneurial Challenges

Let's get specific. Either a generation of entrepreneurs will arise or this lifestyle will end. Very soon, the following must occur:

1. Entrepreneurs must figure out how to cover their own retirement and that of their employees and many others so that when we run out of money for social security and other entitlements it just won't matter.

2. Entrepreneurs must figure out how to compete with the entrepreneurial classes of Brazil, India and other places with less regulation of small business.

3. Entrepreneurs must figure out how to rebuild a strong American industrial base to provide the basic foundational economic strengths of society.

4. Entrepreneurs must figure out how to replace a petroleum-fueled economy with cheaper and hopefully better and cleaner energy alternatives.

5. Entrepreneurs must figure out how to provide inexpensive and quality fresh water, food, mobility and manufacture without cheap oil.

Researchers, experts, professionals, employees and governments do not have the ability to make these things happen. Their contributions will be needed to help accomplish these vital needs, but ultimately it will depend on the skills and creativity of entrepreneurs. These types of changes are the domain of entrepreneurial talents and free enterprise innovations, not of legislative debate, bureaucratic regulation or scholarly discussion. Legislatures, bureaucrats and experts are important to society and are good at certain things, but initiative, innovation, taking calculated risks, and tenacious ingenuity are not their forte. As significant as these challenges are, we need the best of the best solving them.

As entrepreneurs accomplish the goals listed above, we will naturally see increased political stability, a well-funded government that can protect against Chinese or other international aggression, and a narrowing gap between the rich and poor.

It will take a widespread entrepreneurial mindset to figure out how to effectively thwart terrorism without turning the government into a secretive and oppressive surveillance state, and also to help the nation evolve into a less litigious and more productive society. Government cannot effectively undertake either of these projects, since it is a central party to both. And big corporations also have a conflict of interest; with their "fiduciary responsibility to their shareholders," they would naturally use both projects to increase their own power even at the cost of freedom. Entrepreneurs are more suited to succeed in these projects than any other group, and to then promote their solutions with the citizenry.

The most critical problems we now face are also our greatest opportunities. We need more entrepreneurs, and we need entrepreneurs who engage more in social leadership. Our future now, more than at any time since the founding and pioneering eras, depends on producers. Hamilton's ideas contributed much to American growth, but it is time for a renewal of the Jeffersonian spirit of independence and initiative—in all of us.

The Anti-Federalists and Entrepreneurship

Like Gladstone, I believe that the U.S. Constitution is "the greatest work ever struck off by the mind and purpose of man." Even with its notable flaws—especially slavery—it actually provided for the fixing of these flaws. The U.S. Constitution, both directly and indirectly, is responsible for the freedom of more people than any other government document in the world's history.

That said, the anti-Federalists had a point. In fact, they had several. They were mistaken to oppose ratification of the Constitution, but we would be unwise not to listen to the concerns voiced through their loyal opposition. They were right about some critical details. In fact, we are dealing with exactly these concerns today.

Entrepreneurs Change the Debate

The brilliance of both sides of the Constitution debate—the Federalists and the anti-Federalists—is an example of how the producer culture and entrepreneurial mindset accomplish the highest quality in citizen involvement—regardless of party politics. Even in the midst of deeply divided partisan battles, the Federalists and anti-Federalists produced a level of depth, detail, nuance and excellence in citizen debate that is perhaps unsurpassed either before their time or since.

Today's citizen dialogue seldom measures up. I believe the discrepancy is a direct result of the founding generation's lifestyle of entrepreneurship, producer-focused education, ownership, initiative and enterprising mindset. When a nation of entrepreneurs debates on topics of freedom and leadership, the quality is deeper and richer than when lower classes are uninvolved (as in 1780s Britain) or when most citizen-employees are unengaged, preferring to defer to the experts (today's America).

Anti-Federalist Predictions

The anti-Federalists scrutinized the U.S. Constitution and *The Federalist Papers*, and, based on the structures of government, they looked ahead and warned of some of our biggest problems. They also, in most cases, recommended solutions.

What are these challenges, and what can we do about them? To answer both questions, consider six issues the anti-Federalists warned of more than two hundred years ago.

1. The executive branch will increase influence over the national budget.

2. National expenditures will increase and eventually bankrupt the nation.

3. Power will flow consistently away from the states.

4. The courts will eventually have too much power.

5. Justice will be lost as government grows.

6. The treaty power will be abused.

1 The Executive Branch Will Increase Influence Over The National Budget

Anti-Federalist Prediction: The Executive Branch will increase its say over the national budget and then drastically increase debt, run harmful deficits, engage in unconstitutional military actions, and otherwise run the economy toward ruin.

Unfortunately, this has proven to be accurate. We have learned over time that the people don't hold the White House accountable for this behavior because every president blames the last political party (in Congress and the Presidency) for the problem. Both parties use the Executive Branch to commit funding for their projects, even as taxpayers are funding the projects of past administrations.

The Federalists responded to this anti-Federalist warning by correctly pointing out that the Constitution only gives the House of Representatives power over the purse strings. The Federalists' "solution" worked for over a century, but unfortunately for us the Cold War brought secretive and expansive government and the role of the Presidency significantly increased.

Today we are dealing with a system where the House tinkers with and has the final say on national budgets, but where the political environment has turned over to the Presidency responsibility for proposing, gaining the votes for and then administering federal budgets. The House still holds the authority to slow or reject budgets and spending, but it has generally lost the will to use this power. The Executive Branch usually runs the budget.

The result is out-of-control spending. Simple interest payments on the national debt are a huge expense to the taxpayer. Social Security and other entitlement liabilities can never be fully met without continuing in debt and deficits, as well as drastic and progressive increases in taxes.

Both political parties like to blame each other for recessions, unemployment and other economic challenges, but U.S. budgets and spending beyond our means is the underlying problem. As Larry Summers said before he joined the Obama Administration, how can the world's biggest debtor nation remain its biggest power?[19]

Note that China, the second largest economy in the world, has huge savings (unlike the former Soviet Union or the current United States) and is a major buyer of U.S. debt. China has three of the world's four largest banks, the two largest insurance companies and the second largest stock market.[20] With all this, the Communist Party remains in control; it also remains firmly communistic in philosophy[21] and is, if possible, increasingly totalitarian.[22]

China is also expanding what *The Atlantic* called "The Next Empire" in the world: "From oil in Algeria to zinc in Gabon to copper in the Congo, China is muscling in on natural resources all across Africa on a massive scale…. New tracks are being laid, highways built, ports deepened, commercial contracts signed—all on an unprecedented scale, and led by China…Do China's grand designs promise the transformation, at last, of a star-crossed continent? Or merely it's exploitation? To fully grasp China's economic approach in Africa, one must study European imperial history—as Beijing itself has been doing."[23]

As major potential threats like China continue to grow, save, invest and increase their wealth, the U.S. government spends, spends and spends—mostly through debt. In the United States, neither party seems serious about reducing spending. With the Executive Branch running the budgets, spending just keeps increasing. The Reagan Administration greatly increased spending. Presidents Bush, Clinton, Bush and Obama all followed suit—just as predicted by the anti-Federalists.

2 National Expenditures Will Increase

Anti-Federalist Prediction: *Expenditures and taxes will generally increase over time until they bankrupt the nation. They will become massive, and never be significantly reduced.*

This has not yet entirely occurred, but we certainly appear to be on track toward these results. As mentioned, whichever party is in power finds ways to promote more expensive projects while we are still paying off past expenses.

When we allow our representatives to increase the huge U.S. national debt and deficit, we take money out of our own future pockets and those of our children and grandchildren. And let's be clear: The projections on the debts and costs are always understated.

This happens partly because officials make their cost projections based on interest rates projected to be what they have historically been for the U.S., around 3-4%. But this low rate is based at least in part on the perception that the U.S. is a sure bet, that it will never default on its payments. If that perception changes (as it surely will if our spending sprees continue) the rate will go up. Many nations with a less favorable credit rating pay higher interest rates, and the U.S.'s rating is no longer as solid and beyond question as perhaps it once was.

Factor an 8%, 9%, or 12% interest rate into our debt and the cost to our children is astronomical. We may never be able to pay off our debts, and only widespread government programs will keep our citizens afloat if such a scenario occurs—that is, until the government itself can no longer keep up with the demands. While the Treasury Department assures us that this will "never" happen, world lenders seem to be decidedly less confident.[24] Why should the U.S. get the highest credit rating and best rates if its economy isn't producing at the highest and best rate? Our false sense of security on this point is one of the more dangerous faces of the fabled American arrogance.

3 Power Will Flow Away From The States

Anti-Federalist Prediction: Power will flow consistently away from the states and increase the scope, size and power of the federal government.

Again, we are perfectly on target for this even though it has not yet fully matured. Federal budgets now dwarf state costs, and many state programs are funded by federal money. The extent to which this feels "normal" to our citizenry reflects a broad misunderstanding of the type of government under which Americans live, and a reckless contempt for the inherent safeguards that were designed to perpetuate our freedom and autonomy. Indeed, this has become a major misunderstanding in modern America.

The media relentlessly assaults the populace with the message that government is broken—Washington is in gridlock and accomplishes little. In reality, however, this is highly inaccurate. Each year Washington manages to drastically increase the budget, debt and deficit. It is spending more and more annually, and each year Congress authorizes many new programs and empowers more and more oversight, with negligible efforts toward ending obsolete, redundant, ineffective or otherwise unwise projects. A lot is getting done—many would argue too much!

The Senate has killed bills from Republican and Democratic presidents through the years; *but this should be seen as the success of our mixed democratic republic with checks and balances rather than as government not working.* Indeed, even the President relies on the cover of knowing that some policies that he has no authentic desire or intention to implement (but cannot afford the political hit to publicly reject) will be killed on the Hill. If the Senate had killed *more* bills in the past century, the power of the states would not have diminished to such a weakened place.

Both major parties often make the disingenuous mistake of claiming to be carrying out the "democratic" will of the people when they have broad voter support, and then when such support is lacking of blaming the Senate and Congress for gridlock, partisanship and a system that doesn't work. When there is widespread opposition to certain proposed policies, not being able to pass them isn't "gridlock," but *good government.*

The Senate was designed specifically by the founders to protect the states. The idea was to leave most things to the state level and only allow issues to receive federal support when they were wanted by a large majority of Americans and *needed* to be accomplished at the national level.

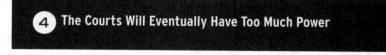

4 The Courts Will Eventually Have Too Much Power

Anti-Federalist Prediction: The courts will not only be independent but will eventually have too much power because there are really no effective checks on their decisions.

This has happened and is still increasing in its impact. Without checks on the Supreme Court, states have little recourse against growing federal controls over powers previously (and constitutionally) held by the states. Our freedoms consistently decrease as the Court expands its interpretation of the role of the federal government in our lives.

5 Justice Will Be Lost as Government Grows

Anti-Federalist Prediction: Governments will become so big and impersonal that even juries won't know or care about the accused; enforcing the rules will be more important than true justice. Freedom will significantly decrease as a result.

This has occurred and is still happening. Before 1895, a jury of peers was not some nominal, demographical designation. The "peers" often actually knew the accused—and even the victim— personally; as a result, they not only were quick to put away those who were truly dangerous to society, but they also used their power to oversee the laws and protect citizens *from government.*

Not only could juries declare someone innocent, they could also nullify laws they considered bad or against freedom. This system was altered at least in part because it was too frequently used in a horrible miscarriage of justice as racist juries ignored the law and both freed white criminals and jailed innocent people from minorities.

It is unfortunate that in response to such abuses we threw out the concept of juries of known peers. In fact, the best remedy for discrimination by the justice system could have been juries of *true* peers, who not only could have protected those falsely accused, but with such empowerment would have been the most motivated to hold accountable the true criminals.

When all are equal before the law and are subject to the admonishment and reprisal of true peers, racism is more readily weeded out. This would have been a great support to abused races, and could have greatly advanced the cause of civil rights in America.

We have never found a way to re-balance this loss of freedom or for the people to quickly overturn the effects of bad laws. California responded within a few years of the 1895 change in jury power by adopting Recalls and Initiatives, but these still left the people with less power than before (they also caused additional problems).

6 The Treaty Power Will Be Abused

Anti-Federalist Prediction: The treaty power will be used to change the Constitution in ways the people don't even know about and that benefit the rich at the cost of the people's freedom.

This has happened and still does. In fact, it may soon be a major concern. For example, when banks fold, endangering entire nations, government can bail them out. The same is true for huge businesses and even State-level governments. But what happens when nations fail financially? The old answer was that they became open to attack like Western Europe during the Great Depression. The result was devastating.

To prevent such a disaster from being repeated, the Allies met in 1944 and crafted the Breton Woods organizations, including the International Monetary Fund and the World Bank. Since then, nations that couldn't pay their debts have been bailed out by the IMF.

In return for such benefits, the borrowing nation submits to "Austerity Measures," under which the IMF closely watches national policy and government institutions to ensure that the nation does nothing to jeopardize its ability to pay back its loans. This system has certainly had its share of successes. But Austerity also amounts to a virtual transfer of sovereignty from national government to IMF regulators—well beyond the power of the citizenry to require accountability or to effect remedies.

So far the United States and most Western European nations have been lenders to the IMF, not debtors. But if the U.S. ever needed to become a debtor nation, Austerity Measures would prove the anti-Federalist prediction devastatingly true.

For example, when Greece defaulted on its debt payments in early 2010 and Spain threatened to do the same, the European Union came to the rescue. The IMF was called in to advise the EU, and Austerity was established over the Greek government. Many citizens (including a great number of professionals and managers) took to the streets in protest. But instead of protesting a drastic loss of freedom under Austerity, they were complaining about wage freezes.[25]

There are three ways the U.S. can avoid Austerity at some point in the future. First, we can tighten our belts, reduce government expenditures, and deregulate and lower taxes on small business (which historically make up 80% of our economy's growth). This would convince and enable many employers to hire, and consumers to spend.

Second, we could borrow from other nations. China has a huge surplus of government and also private savings, and it wants to invest in the United States. Indeed it is our largest creditor now. Other nations may also be persuaded to keep supporting our spending habits. But one has to wonder why our philosophical opponent (communist China) wants to invest so much. Are its motives pure? What if they're not? Is it a simple profit motive? What if it's something more?

As Peggy Noonan wrote in *The Wall Street Journal*: "People are freshly aware of the real-world implications of a $1.6 trillion deficit, of a $14 trillion debt. It will rob America of its economic power, and eventually even of its ability to defend itself. Militaries cost money. And if other countries own our debt, don't they in some new way own us? If China holds enough of your paper, does it also own some of your foreign policy? Do we want to find out?"[26]

A third possible method of solving our debt problem is to borrow from huge international corporations. This carries the same problems as borrowing from nations.

Note that if we do eventually take IMF loans, they will only pay the *interest* on the debts. We will have to pay back the original loans, and an international team of regulators will run our national economic policy and make our economic decisions. If Americans are frustrated with Congress, imagine their frustration with a group of international bank officials running our economy—bankers who may not have as their motive either to see us out of debt to them or to strengthen our economy, society, international influence or other elements of our way of life.

The rule of international borrowing is simple: The lenders make the rules. Method One of facing our economic reality—returning to an incentivizing free enterprise system and living within our means—is hard. Neither political party wants to promote it, and whoever does implement it will probably be blamed for higher short-term unemployment, stock market losses and economic recession. In the long term, however, this course will revitalize America's economy and free lifestyle.

The other two options keep America in economic decline and will eventually result in reduced political power, weaker national security and fallen status. They will also, most importantly, lead to a significant decrease in our freedoms and the prosperity of our children and grandchildren.

This is our choice: Make the tough decisions now, or lose freedoms and prosperity for generations. So far we have passed on making the right choice. No wonder independents, tea partyists and the far left are so frustrated with both Republicans and Democrats.

Moreover, economic downturns are three-headed dragons; and to this point we have only faced recession and high unemployment. Inflation could be the next crisis, and it could very well rekindle and inflame the first two.[27]

Whatever we decide to do economically, we should, like the Federalists and anti-Federalists, clearly understand one thing: Economics and Freedom are directly linked. A debtor nation is less free than a solvent one.

Solutions Old and New

The anti-Federalist and other proposed solutions for these problems may well have helped:

- The Bill of Rights would include the requirement that juries consist of local peers who know the accused and can protect citizens from government.

- Treaties would require full debate in and passage by Congress—just like laws.

- Any decision by the Supreme Court could be overridden by a majority of the States.

How effective these amendments would have been is debatable. But the answer may be found in a proposed anti-Federalist amendment that actually did get passed. To counter the danger of huge expenditures and taxes by the Executive Branch, loss of power from the House to the Presidency, and transfer of powers from the States to the federal government, the anti-Federalists wanted an amendment clearly stating that all power not specifically given by the Constitution to the federal government would be retained by the states.

The anti-Federalists got their way in the ratification of the Tenth Amendment: "The powers not delegated to the United States by the Constitution, nor prohibited to it by the states, are reserved to the states respectively, or to the people."

Unfortunately, these were weakened by Court cases between 1803 and 1820, and later by treaties adopted between 1944 and 2001.

We The People

It turns out that Constitutional limits and language are only guaranteed to last as long as the people are vigilantly involved. No matter what the Constitution says, it won't endure if the people don't closely read it and demand that it be followed. In this sense they are the fourth branch of government: The Overseers.

When the people, for whatever reasons, stop requiring officials and experts to adhere to the Constitution, those in power alter the Constitution, redefine its precepts, and sometimes mutually agree upon a revisionist and opportunistic definition of its language. The people are left out of the process, and their freedoms decrease.

At times, as designed, Constitutional checks and balances keep one Branch from usurping power even if the people aren't involved. But the greater danger occurs when a collusion of Branches agree in taking away power from the States or the people (this happens too often, especially since *Butler v. the United States* in 1936).

Arguably the most important document for freedom ever created by mankind was established and ratified by those who supported the U.S. Constitution. The second deepest freedom analysis of government was provided by their enemies, the anti-Federalists. This opposing group knew that no matter what a Constitution says (as important as the language and forms certainly are), the people simply must stay actively involved or they will inevitably see their freedoms decline.

Live Long and Prosper: The Entrepreneurial Mindset

The fact that both the Federalists and the anti-Federalists came from a society of owners and producers is neither surprising nor irrelevant. Owners value freedom over security; they see the most decorated experts and celebrities as merely other citizens; and see their own role as a citizen as vital to society. Producers think in terms of protecting society's freedoms, and they simply don't believe this responsibility should ever be delegated or neglected.

Successful ownership and entrepreneurship are all about keeping track of all the details; taking action whenever it is needed to achieve the desired results; listening to the counsel of experts and authorities—and then leading by making the best decisions even when such decisions go against expert advice; and building effective teams that work together without depending too much on those at the top. People immersed in such values and experienced in such skills are truly competent in handling and preserving freedom.

What we need in our day is not necessarily more specific proposals from the Federalists or anti-Federalists, but rather a return to the producer-entrepreneurial style of thinking and expertise that founded and built the freest nation in history. If we want a society of freedom that endures and prospers, we must as citizens become talented and practiced in the arts of freedom. America was created on the basis of freedom, and until we choose to become a citizenry steeped in freedom principles and actively involved in their promotion, freedom will not likely increase.

Get Back in Line!

Virtually every child looks forward to the freedoms and responsibilities of being an adult. Liberty is a blessing of maturity, and a free society is only maintained by a culture of adults. While this may be obvious, it has become a challenge in our day. The term "adult" has come to be commonly defined as anyone above a certain age—and has largely lost its qualitative nuance; but of course not all people older than 21 are free.

True adulthood requires more than maintaining a heartbeat for two or more decades. To achieve and perpetuate freedom, societies need a culture that celebrates and manifests the responsibilities and leadership of adulthood.

This is more difficult to achieve than first meets the eye. When the general culture isn't up to freedom standards, it is easy for people to go along with the norm. Indeed, one reason freedom is so truly rare in history is the difficulty of changing cultural norms. Let's consider several cultures that have widespread influence today.

Elementary Culture

The culture of grade schools has huge impact beyond the schoolyard. Elementary Culture values the following:

- staying in the good graces of those above you, especially the authorities

- reliance on experts
- dependence on basic needs and remedies being provided
- playing
- having good toys
- learning and following the rules
- getting rewards from the authorities by meeting their expectations

As good as these things may be for classroom and playground management, they are less enchanting as the cultural underpinnings of adult neighborhoods, towns, cities and nations. Free citizens are not exactly marked by their desire to please government authorities or being dependent on state programs. Nor is liberty positively promoted when the citizens focus mostly on play, getting the best toys in life (from cars to computers to vacations), or seeking rewards from upper classes or government officials.

Obviously order and cooperation are desirable shared values in a society; but there is a huge difference between free citizens who have a significant say in establishing the rules and dependent citizens who are hardly involved in governance.

One of the great heroic roles in our modern culture is found in elementary teachers who work, serve and sacrifice to help raise and (hopefully) educate the next generation. For example, 63% of public grade-school teachers spend their own money buying food for at least one hungry student each month.[28] This stunning statistic shows much of what is right, and wrong, with modern America. The individual voluntarism and selfless service by such teachers is a foundation of freedom. When parents don't own their responsibility to care for their children (which is the case in at least some, perhaps many, of these cases), our moral imperatives demand that adults must. And when "adults" act and even become helpless, like children, the state steps forward to feed and care for them.

Think of the great freedom cultures of history—from the Hebrew and Greek golden ages to the free Saracens, Swiss, English and early Americans, among others. These citizens were not dependents and were not particularly interested in pleasing the "authorities." In fact, they held the government dependent on the people and required government officials to please the citizens. They made family and work the center of adult life, as opposed to the "bread and circuses" of Elementary Cultures in Rome and other less-than-free societies.

High School Culture

Some adults live more in a High School Culture that, like Elementary Culture, does not promote free society. High School Culture generally values the following:

- fitting in
- popularity
- sports
- cliques
- class systems
- disconnection from adult society

Sometimes even teachers side or identify with certain cliques and basically join this culture. When applied to adult society, this creates a culture that hardly deserves and never maintains freedom. In many towns, for example, high school glory days represent all that is right and good, and success in sports is equated with success in life.

There are three major types of life success in High School Culture: 1) doing well in school and sports, 2) raising children who do well in school and sports, and 3) having grandchildren who are succeeding in school and sports. This is High School Culture indeed. In fact, in many places the activities of the local high school are the actual focal point and highest expression of community culture and family connectedness.

This happens in many traditionally conservative cultures such as many small and mid-size towns, much of the American West, Texas and the plains states, and also in traditionally liberal populations like in the South, the Appalachians and the Midwest. There are corresponding regional blocks in Canada.

Whatever they call themselves politically, the dominant culture in such places often centers on the high school and reflects high school values. Adults living High School Culture focus on their local and private issues and hope to ignore political society until it forces itself into their lives. At such times, the typical response is resentment and rebellion.

Unfortunately for freedom, seeking to fit in/be popular, join the best clique and thereby win the caste battle, and stay as disconnected from politics as possible, do not tend to promote free society. Whether or not these pursuits are good for youth warrants discussion; but they are certainly not foundations of liberty or the ideal goals of free adults.

College-Corporate Culture

Nor is College-Corporate Culture naturally supportive of freedom. Just as high school usually has more freedoms than elementary, college and work culture sometimes feels free in comparison to high school society. College-Corporate Culture is usually more dominant in bigger cities than in small towns (though of course there are people from all cultures living almost everywhere, who tend to coalesce into micro-pods that reflect their values). College-Corporate Culture values the following:

• personal success

• career preparation and advancement

• non-committal relationships

• entertainment

• status

- pursuing individual interests

- spending on lifestyle

People and places that adopt College-Corporate values experience more personal freedom than citizens living elementary or high school lifestyles. But they are unable to establish or maintain freedom on the large scale over time—and they usually do not concern themselves with trying. "Me" and "I" dominate the perspectives of Elementary, High School and College-Corporate Cultures.

Official Culture

In elementary and high schools there are principals, administrators, teachers and other officials who take care of the little people. In the adult lives that mirror grade and high schools, regular citizens see themselves as being taken care of by officials and the officers see themselves as taking care of the people. Since they value class systems and popularity, the people tend to acquiesce to those they consider "in charge." Many even feel resentment towards those who seem to rebel against the ("adult") officials. Woodstockers, John Birchers, the "-ism" extremists and other "rebels" are seen like druggies, gangsters and other unsavory high school cliques. The "good" kids don't fight the system.

College, university and corporate officials are often seen as distant, professionally- rather than personally-interested, upper class, and probably self-serving. "They ignore us, and we ignore them," is the operating principle of the regular people. "We're too busy pursuing our own success and fun to worry about them anyway—except to impress them." The officers, in contrast, see the regular people as functionaries to help them achieve big goals and successes for the good of all.

Official Culture values the following:

- respect of those in authority

- people following the rules

- the infallibility of the rules
- the need to lead significant, bold change
- progress overcoming the roadblocks which the regular people naively call "freedom"
- keeping the system strong
- promoting support and respect for the system
- really helping the people
- giving the people what they really need, even if they "think" they don't want it or understand how much they need it

These have little likelihood of promoting long-term freedom. Note that the official value of really helping the people is nearly always truly sincere; they really mean it. While some may consider this patronizing, like the *noblesse oblige* of upper classes, we can still give due credit to those who genuinely seek to serve and help people.

For Official Culture to flourish, many of the population must live Elementary or High School Culture. This requires an attachment to popularity and celebrity. The regular people must see celebrities as special, deserving of special benefits.

Such people are easily swayed by charisma.

In contrast, the American founders specifically arranged our government with separations, checks and balances in order to avoid the power of such childish charisma (see, for example, Federalist 1, 10, 67 and 68), which they considered very dangerous based on the histories of Greece and especially Rome. Einstein was right: "A foolish faith in authority is the worst enemy of truth."

For freedom to succeed the majority of the people must move beyond being cared for by experts and instead adopt and live in Adult Culture. Freedom is lost in cultures dominated by Official Culture. For that matter, freedom cannot survive in a society run by Elementary, High School, College-Corporate and/or Official values and systems.

Adult Culture

As mentioned above, freedom is incredibly rare in history. It occurs only with an extremely high cost in resources, blood, sacrifice and wisdom, and it is maintained only when the citizenry does its job of truly leading the nation as Overseers. Regular people must understand what is going on at the same or a higher level than government leaders, or the leaders become an upper class and the people are relegated to following child-like as submissives and dependents.

To elect the right leaders and support the right direction in government, the people must study, watch, analyze and think deeply. They must study and understand the principles of freedom, and they must get involved to ensure that these principles are correctly applied.

Adult Culture values those things that keep societies free, prosperous and happy. Such values include:

- being your genuine self—and therefore not easily swayed by peers, experts or anyone else
- actively and voluntarily contributing to society's needs
- accepting responsibility for society and its future
- appropriately and maturely making a positive difference in the world
- accepting others for who they are and respecting their contributions
- spending wisely
- balancing spending with appropriate savings and investment
- consistently saving and effectively investing for the future
- dedicating yourself to committed relationships
- helping the young learn and progress
- providing principled and effective assistance to those in need
- influencing the rules, policies and laws to be what they should be, changing bad ones, and following the good ones

- sacrificing yourself for important things when it is right
- taking risks when they are right
- respecting those in authority, earning and expecting their respect in return, and holding them accountable to their proper roles and duties
- balancing relationships and work with appropriate leisure, entertainments, sports, toys, hobbies and/or relaxation
- openly discouraging and if needed fighting class systems and unprincipled/unjust inequalities
- helping influence positive change while keeping the things which are positively working
- never allowing "progress" to trample freedoms
- promoting support for and respect of the system as long as it is positive and improving
- really, sincerely helping the people while respecting them as adults, individuals and citizens worthy of admiration and esteem

Any move away from these adult values is a step toward less freedom. And let's be clear: Most people naturally want to be treated like adults. For example, there are now more "independents" than Republicans or Democrats—in part because the political parties so often seem to exhibit elementary and high school values.

Populist movements nearly always arise when governments seem to adopt Official Culture. The anti-Washington populism which swept President Obama into office was largely a response to perceived officiousness by President Bush and Vice President Cheney, just as Tea Party populism arose when many felt that the Obama Administration was treating regular Americans like inferiors.

Any sense of arrogance, superiority, smugness or overwhelming and unresponsive mandate by political leaders quite predictably spurs frustrated reactions. Both parties routinely fall short in this arena, however, as do many in non-public sectors. All of us would do well to guard ourselves against hubris and pride, which are perhaps the most negative of High School values. When combined with the harmful College-Corporate values of pushy ambition and myopic self-centeredness, they wreak havoc on societal leadership, prosperity and freedom. Instead, adult societies value relaxed confidence, poise, genuine humility, and authentic strength.

Adult Culture benefits from such values as elementary sharing and playing, high school enthusiasm and idealism, college self-improvement and dedicated learning, corporate hard work and excellence, and official emphasis on the rule of law and authentic caring for others. However, each of these is optimized and put in context in an Adult society—the only culture that can synthesize a meaningful and constructive complex culture to build and re-tain lasting freedom.

The Hidden War

Sadly, High School and College Culture have created a war brewing between the generations. This is not a generation gap or a simple matter of the old not understanding the young. It is an actual financial war on today's children by their parents and grandparents. But the youth aren't engaged—they are simply the victims.

Former Reagan speechwriter Peggy Noonan wrote in *The Wall Street Journal*:

> "And there are the moral implications of the debt, which have so roused the tea party movement: The old vote themselves benefits that their children will have to pay for. What kind of people do that?"[29]

Certainly not those with adult values.

As *The Economist* put it:

> "There is an unvoiced contract that binds the generations. Parents look after their children, with a view to helping them do at least as well as they themselves have done, and grown-up children look after their parents, in the hope that their children will do the same for them one day. But there is now a 'breakdown in the balance between the generations....'

> "Mr. Willetts cites, approvingly, the way some American Indian tribal councils used to take decisions in the light of how they would affect the next several generations. In Britain, alas, it is painfully hard to see beyond the next election."[30]

The same problems are widespread in the United States. The tribal approach mentioned clearly comes from a society with adult values, unlike the philosophy guiding much of Anglo-American financial policy.

No Chewing Gum!

Besides self-centeredness, another high school value is that the "good" people always follow the officials. John Dewey taught that the most lasting lessons learned in schools are the non-academic cultural values taught. While it has been famously said that all one ever needs to know he learns in kindergarten,[31] one lesson that seems most to have taken hold is that the teacher (or president, expert or agent) is always right. This intellectually oppressive lie has always been the death of freedom.

Consider how recessionary times impacted the generation of youth born between 1980 and 2000 and raised with jobs as the central goals of their life. They know how to stay in line, not chew gum in class, stick to their social clique, and leave decision-making to the officials. But not only have innovation and leadership not been highly rewarded in their lives, they are alien to most of them. Speaking of this generation of college graduates, the experts wrote:

> "You'd think if people are more individualistic, they'd be more independent. But it's not really true. There's an element of entitlement—they expect people to figure things out for them."[32]

> In the workplace, they "need almost constant direction…. Many flounder without precise guidelines but thrive in structured situations that provide clearly defined rules."[33]

> "This is a group that's done resume building since middle school. They've been told they've been preparing to go out and do great things after college. And now they've been dealt a 180 [by high unemployment rates].[34]

> "Trained through childhood to disconnect performance from reward, and told repeatedly that they are destined for great things, many are quick to place blame elsewhere when something goes wrong, and inclined to believe that bad situations will…be sorted out by parents or other helpers."[35]

Millennials, the Net Generation, Generation Y, or the Digital Natives as some call the generation born between 1981 and 2001[36] do not like conflict, are an "On Demand generation" that wants everything now, and "are used to getting what they want instantly or close to it…."[37]

They don't like having to initiate things and they have a "need for constant feedback about themselves."[38]

One study found that "…internet users aged 18-24 were the least likely of all age groups to e-mail a public official or make an on-line political donation. But when it came to using the web to share political news or join political causes on social networks, they were far ahead of everyone else…to broadcast their activism to their peers."[39]

Millennials are supremely confident about their future, want above all to be good parents, have good marriages and use their careers to do good, but expect these things to happen with little work and are used to giving up if things don't go the way they expect.[40]

"All of these characteristics are worrisome, given a harsh economic environment that requires perseverance, adaptability, humility, and entrepreneurialism."[41]

A generation of conveyor-belt education has failed to prepare most of today's youth for the real world. This same generation has many very positive traits, however, including being pleasant, cheerful, helpful, ambitious, family-oriented, optimistic, obedient, idealistic, inclusive and tolerant.[42] They are also very numerous. Where the famously populous boomer generation boasted 79 million people in America, there are over 100 million Millennials.[43]

Perhaps most positively for the future of freedom, interest in entrepreneurial careers is more popular with this generation than with their parents or grandparents. The simple solution for the Millennials, and for a lot of other people, is more jobs. This requires more entrepreneurial action.

Entrepreneurship requires adult values, not people full of high-school risk aversion and dependence.

Today we need a wholesale return to the adult values in our society. Insecurely seeking to fit in, searching for popularity/sports/toys as the measure of success, dependency on government and officials, class systems, pleasing those in charge, waiting for others to structure your success, feeling entitled, thinking your resume should ensure success, expecting a lottery or reality TV show to bail you out, and blaming others when things go wrong—these are not ideals free people cherish.

The question for our generation is: Can we regain our freedoms without putting aside childish things and becoming a society of adults?

Robin Hood or Prince John?

When the government takes middle-class tax money and bails out big bankers, automobile manufacturers and other big businesses paying out huge multi-million dollar bonuses, that's not socialism. Socialism, like Robin Hood, proposes to take money from the middle and upper classes and redistribute it to the poor. But during the Great Recession, the lower and lower-middle classes found it much harder to make ends meet. Many lost their jobs, and even their homes.

Where was Robin Hood when they needed him? Where was *their* socialist bailout?

Whether or not you subscribe to the socialist ideal (and I decidedly do not), a careful consideration of the social and economic climate of the U.S. is warranted. What is really happening? Conservative talk radio and television hosts have railed about the "rise of socialism"; but in reality something else is going on here.

When socialistic programs are introduced, the lower classes benefit and the upper-middle and upper classes pay the bill. But in our time, *precisely the opposite* has happened. In addition to increasing woes for the lower and lower-middle classes, the upper classes actually *benefited* from the economic downturn. The number of millionaires grew 16%[44] during the Great Recession of 2008-2009, and those with a net worth over $5 million grew 17%.[45]

So why did conservatives and Tea Partyists bandy about the S-word so much? And after all is said and done, what difference does it make what we call it?

While the "socialism" furor may have been linked to the Health Care debate and other left-of-center policies and proposals of the Obama Administration, a deeper look shows that socialism is not the real culprit. It is critical to understand that this distinction is not just a talking point for politicians and pundits to discuss on Sunday morning talk shows, or for academics and intellectuals to publish in scholarly journals.

By misdiagnosing the problem, we are also applying the wrong remedies and can never hope for improvement. We are all the day vigilant against the small-time con of Robin Hood, while Prince John plunders us in our sleep.

What is Socialism?

The technical definition of socialism is government ownership of the major means of production in a society. American Liberalism, in contrast, believes that there should be both a private and a government sector, and that the government should highly tax and regulate the private sector. While both of these are anti-conservative, they are not one and the same, and the difference is critical.

American Liberalism does believe in limits, checks and balances; it believes in a separate private sector. Socialism believes in none of these; it believes that the government should run the entire economy. Obama Administration involvement in bailing out banks and auto companies certainly had liberal overtones, but the top banks quickly paid back government loans and went back to private ownership.

In this sense, to label this as socialistic is not accurate. Again: this is not a question of semantics, but speaks to the very heart of the issue.

In the wake of the economic meltdown of the twenty-aughts and early twenty-tens, the government drastically increased regulations on large and small businesses. This regulatory activity is a basic value and tool of liberalism. While liberalism seeks to ever increase regulation on private businesses, socialism seeks to own most and eventually all the companies in a nation. Polls showed the Obama Administration to be left of the American populace in regard to fiscal and other types of regulations, but all within liberal rather than socialistic definitions.

It may be well argued that this distinction is simply a question of degrees; but even in that paradigm the differences demand a greater understanding of and tailored responses to the liberal and socialist encroachments on freedom and prosperity.

If It Quacks Like A Duck...

Another reason many called Great Recession policies "socialist" is that government actions caused private businesses to shed employees at the same time that the government was hiring. When the media shared the numbers showing that average private salaries are less than the average government employees make, the "socialism" name-calling was a natural angry response. *The Economist* predicted growing political battles between taxpayers and government employees in nearly all nations.[46]

We need to get serious about incentivizing small and mid-size businesses. Many of the government programs and regulations started during the Great Recession actually made it much harder for small businesses to succeed and grow. How, exactly, does this help unemployment?

In fact, it dis-incentivizes entrepreneurship and hiring, and encourages people to go on government programs. This certainly *feels* like socialism.

And big business is facing similar challenges. For example, Intel's chief executive Paul Otellini said that the U.S. is driving away businesses and employers:

> "The things that are not conducive to investments here are taxes and capital investment credits. A new semiconductor factory at world scale built from scratch is about $4.5 billion—in the United States. If I build that factory in almost any other country in the world, where they have significant incentive programs, I could save $1 billion."[47]

How many jobs are we sending to other countries because of our high taxes and regulations?

This was clearly not a hypothetical situation; Intel built its latest factory in China. Said Otellini:

> "And it wasn't because of the labor costs either. Yeah, the construction costs were a little bit lower, but the cost of operating when you look at it after tax was substantially lower…"[48]

What does it mean when China's communist business environment is more inviting to U.S. companies, more conducive to their growth, than the United States? When the regulations and taxes in the U.S. make doing business *in China* attractive? The U.S. now ranks #40 out of forty industrialized nations in appeal to business.[49] It's almost as if the U.S. government doesn't *want* business to succeed or grow, and only thinks that government spending and government jobs are the solutions to economic challenges.

This is easy prey for conspiracy hunters, but I don't think Washington is capable either of such ubiquitous cleverness or such cooperation. I think it is much more likely that, when it comes to preserving freedom, they are simply not minding the store. Other pressing needs have our leaders distracted, and the expedient responses they turn to also happen to militate against our future freedom and prosperity—and specifically, against free enterprise.

No wonder so many people are angry at recent presidential administrations. No wonder so many have cried "socialism." How can we defend against the allegation that our government purposely wants private businesses to fail or flee the U.S.? Instead of promoting incentives that bring more business and jobs, the government has promoted higher taxes and regulations like health care that make business success *more* difficult.

More government regulation, increased government hiring and increased government social programs demanding ever-higher taxes: these are features not only of liberal policies, but of a growing aristocracy.

Socialism *versus* Aristocracy

Predictably, most Americans today who actually have an opinion on the matter readily conjure the twentieth-century enemy of free enterprise—Socialism—rather than the older, forgotten eighteenth- and nineteenth-century evil of aristocratic rule. But the fact that lower classes are struggling more than ever while the upper classes are increasing their wealth during economic downturns is a clear sign that aristocracy *is* the issue.

Consider this: in socialist cultures celebrity and fame are denigrated; in aristocratic societies they are esteemed and celebrated. We clearly love celebrity at levels far beyond socialistic, conservative or even liberal societies. Aristocracies and monarchies are the domain of such infatuation with fame, get-rich-quick schemes and the lottery mentality. Like Shakespeare's Antonio, we just *know* our ship is about to come in.

Conservatives traditionally invest in building businesses and like-minded community; liberals in educational degrees, professional excellence and credibility; and socialists in government positions. Like characters in an Austen novel, those in the lower classes of an aristocracy fantasize about some punctuated leap in their "prospects"—from marrying a rich and well-connected suitor to the modern equivalent of winning on Survivor, American Idol, The Amazing Race, The Bachelor or some other concocted scenario where the fate of the aspirants largely lies with those in power and the caprice of fate. Note that in real pyramid schemes there are a few winners at the top but thousands of hopeful and willing enablers the rest of the way down.

Why the Difference Matters

The debate between socialism and aristocracy is more than just semantical.

The technically inaccurate label of socialism allows the educated media and the elite establishment to patronize and condescend to the "uneducated" that push for change. It allows government officials to dismiss the "uncouth dissenters" while maintaining their conviction that *"they"* [the "educated," the most "talented," most "intelligent" ones] *know what the nation needs and those whose opinion really matters* [the "educated," the most "talented," most "intelligent" ones] *are completely in favor of their proposals.*

Unfortunately, those citizens who put aside apathy and stand up to make a difference find themselves always frustrated because they fight the wrong battle. If socialism is our problem, the perpetrator is the political leaders promoting socialist policies, and the philosophical left is to blame. But if aristocracy is the challenge, then the two parties are *both* culprits in the promotion of a privileged class; if aristocracy is the challenge, the citizen is his own worst enemy as he does not pay the price to rise above the mediocre education of our schools or to see beyond a complicit, dumbed-down media designed more for entertainment value and advertising revenue than positive impact on freedom and prosperity.

If we think socialism is the enemy, we will put our effort into electing different leaders, only to discover that Washington's problems continue and increase *no matter whom we elect*. By misdiagnosing the problem, we are using the wrong treatments and failing to get better.

No matter how active and engaged voters are—from the left or the right or the middle—if we continue to think that either socialism or capitalism is our problem then all our efforts will continue to be impotent. Very little will change in Washington and our problems will continue to grow.

Virile and Viral

If we realize, in contrast, that aristocracy is the real problem and that electing a ruling upper class from either party will only worsen the problem, we can shift focus and consider what is really needed. And the answer, the real solution, will become clear: As long as we live in a society of upper and lower classes, our freedoms and our opportunities for prosperity will continue to decline.

The solution is not to just elect a different leader, but for all American citizens to once again obtain the kind of education that allowed regular farmers and shop-keepers to study *The Federalist Papers* and listen to and consider eight-hour debates during the Lincoln-Douglass era.

If we think the problem is socialism, we will consider great education benign and ineffectual. But if we know the real problem—that people in both parties and in all social strata are enabling a growing aristocratic power over our society—then we will realize that simply electing a better Senator or President is not nearly enough of a solution.

True: Socialism and aristocracy share many symptoms, so electing the best leaders is still vitally important to stem encroachments on our freedom and way of life. And the threat of "socialism" is a lot sexier to media outlets seeking ratings. But the real issue, the unseen issue, is aristocracy.[50] And until the American people realize this and more of us get the same quality of education as the CEOs, Judges and Presidents, the problems will continue to grow. More than any other factor, it is education that determines class levels.

This doesn't mean that we need all enroll in the Ivy League. In truth, the greatest classics of history are still the true library of freedom, wealth and leadership. Virtually every county library has the great texts of liberty and success available.

The question is, do Americans value our freedom enough to end the rise of aristocratic rule by becoming greatly educated ourselves? Will we develop our innate genius and rise, as Jefferson predicted, to be the natural aristocracy over which no despot could rule? Will we step up to our responsibilities as citizens and qualify ourselves for our role as the overseers of government by learning about freedom, leadership, economics, human nature and the other great ideas of mankind?

As our society is on track for disaster from numerous threats (to our food supply, availability of fuel, decaying infrastructure, dependency on programs that have poor prospects for future funding, terrorism, failing economy) we all know that somebody needs to *"Do something!"*

We have been caught in the binary trap of either expecting someone else to "fix it" or expecting that we can make a difference just by making our voices heard. But our moral authority and our ability to impact our society's direction will come not from complaining about the ideas or performance of those who have stepped up to lead, but from actually *having* the answers to society's ills. We can't just protest that the world simply *must* turn back the clock two hundred years. New leadership—leadership of the character, competence and quality of the founding generation—is needed of today's American citizens.

If we truly revere the American founders and celebrate their accomplishments, we must move beyond hero worship and Constitutional groupie-ism (of either the right or left varieties) and actually *do as the founders did:* we must apply a profound understanding of sound principles to the establishment of policies and forms that directly apply to our complex and critical situation *today.*

This we can do, just as the American founders did in their day. As I have said elsewhere: Getting a world-class education and running successful businesses *is* "doing something." It is my opinion that it is precisely the "something" that is called for today, and that any other solution which does not include a better-educated populace of independent thinkers has a different outcome than liberty and justice for all.

It is time for an entrepreneurial approach to getting an individualized, superb, great, innovative leadership education in the classics. Each of us can do it, and the future of our freedoms depends upon it. It is time for a revolution of entrepreneurs who stop waiting for expert fixes and set out to fix the world themselves— one entrepreneurial venture at a time.

If the current growth of American aristocracy is allowed to continue, our future is destined to be less free and more harshly lacking in opportunity than any socialistic society. The criticism of "socialism" is certainly negative; but unless we change course, the aristocracy that our grandchildren and their children inherit will be something far worse.

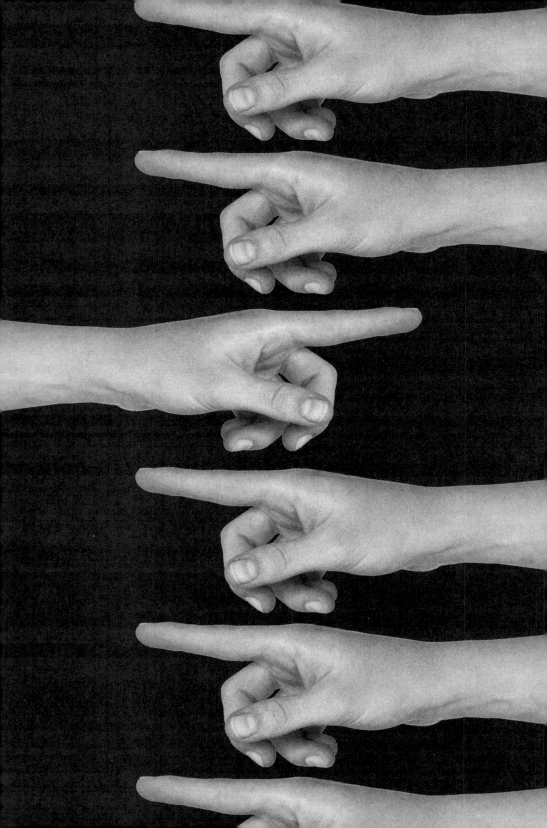

Rise of the Independents

Americans have forgotten what brings freedom. It is not political parties, which most often vacillate between ineffective argument and cooperative regulations that reduce freedom. Indeed, freedom and prosperity occur only when the regular citizenry gets actively involved in promoting true liberty.

The rise of independents is involving increasingly more citizens in the daily political process and overriding the monopoly of the two parties. Whether you agree or disagree with the independents, they are changing the future of freedom.

But who are these independents, what do they really believe in, and what is their future? The answers may surprise you.

How to Really Understand the Issues

If you want to understand and profit from the political, economic and cultural forces at play in today's world, you must understand two things:

1. The evolution of pre-modernism, modernism and post-modernism.

2. How independents view and are shaping the world.

Armed with this understanding you'll be able to see through the superficial and misleading "liberal *versus* conservative" debate portrayed by the media. Furthermore, you'll be able to harness our current societal transformations to your advantage.

The most fundamental question in the Great Debate of how society should be organized is "Who (or what) will save us?"

Pre-modernism, modernism, and post-modernism all have different answers.

Pre-Modernism & Modernism

Modernism is defined in many ways. One of the most enlightening comes by comparing modernism to the pre-modern and post-modern worlds. Philosophy is not everyone's cup of tea, but I hope you'll entertain a little philosophical discussion because I think it's really important to the future of our freedoms.

The value of this discussion is in understanding how man understands himself in the context of community, and in his view of the proper role of government.

In a nutshell, pre-modern societies believe that some supernatural being (or super-powerful entity) will save mankind. Man is flawed and weak (so the narrative goes), and if he is to be saved it must come from something greater than man.

The three main branches of this view—one God, many gods, and shamanic energy powers—all agree on the basics:

• man needs saving

• he can't save himself

• a higher power must save us

• we should therefore live in a way that pleases or avails us of the benefits of the higher power

That's a simple version of pre-modernism.

Modernism begins when a society changes these assumptions. In the West, the modern era adopted the following beliefs:

• man needs saving

• he can't save himself

• it seems no godlike power is inclined to step up (for whatever reason)

• so man must build institutions which can save him

In short, modernism rests on the belief that man-made institutions can and should save us.

The early modernists built on their pre-modern religious roots and turned to churches as the institutions most likely to fix the world's problems. Those who were dissatisfied or impatient with this solution eventually turned to governments as the answer. If there are any problems in the world (according to this view), government should fix them. If a government won't fix a problem or allows any suffering, it is bad and should be reformed or replaced. If a government tries but can't fix problems, it is too weak and must be given more power.

After all, we humans like our higher powers incredibly strong—and always benevolent.

Government *versus* Markets

A third major branch of modernism arose when governments repeatedly failed to solve the world's problems. This school of thought believed that big business was the answer. Huge, powerful businesses, as Keynes argued, reach a size where they care less about profit and more about taking care of their employees and society in general.[51]

This view has business provide insurance, benefits and other perks to help the people live happily. It tends to ignore small business and even large "greedy" businesses, and instead promotes more responsibility from the biggest corporations.

In recent years we've witnessed the debates between all three branches of modernism, from faith-based initiatives (church as central institution) to health care reform (government as central institution) to executive bonuses (corporation as central institution). But since the media usually couches all these and many other issues in "Conservative *versus* Liberal" terms, few people realize what is actually going on in these controversies.

The church-as-savior belief lost most of its influence in the last century, leaving governments and businesses to jockey for first place in this race to be the central institution of mankind's allegiance.

Many participated in this debate: Marx, Darwin, Bastiat, Nietzsche, Freud, C.S. Lewis, Andrew Carnegie, Ayn Rand, Solzhenitsyn, Keynes, Kinsey, Milton Friedman, Mao, Reagan, Clinton, Bush, Obama, several Popes, Bill Gates, Warren Buffett and others.

The Current Debate

Ralph Nader has argued that the only solution to our current problems is for the super-rich to use their influence and power to reduce corporate dominance in the world and allow governments to save us. Government offers the most hope to mankind, this view argues, and corporations are the problem. Greedy corporations cause economic downturns, according to this view.

In contrast, the famous Shell Oil Scenarios have made a case that government cannot and will not solve truly global problems like energy, environment, transportation, economic ups and downs, communication and education. Their solution is for corporations with experience in planning across borders to be given the power to make and follow a "blueprint" for global success.

Leaving it to governments would cause a mad "scramble" toward more war, poverty, depression and suffering, according to this view. After all, the corporations say, when the economy falls it hurts most companies and nearly all governments. Only the biggest corporations remain strong—*so they should govern us!*

Both sides ("Government Fix It" and "Big Business as Savior") see the other as a dangerous utopian scheme. Consider, for example, the issue of health care (or energy policy, unemployment, boosting the economy, or any other national issue). Most officials and media personnel see the debates as political, between conservatives and liberals. To a certain extent—votes in Congress—this is true. But the real debate is much deeper and broader than politics.

It is about who we are as human beings and where we are headed as a society. While there are still some supporters of pre-modern or modern views, governments and businesses have so far failed to deliver heaven on earth or even ideal society.

The End of Conservative *versus* Liberal

For most people today, neither of these institutions are the answer. When conservatives talk about faith-based initiatives or Republicans tout trickle-down economics, most people are skeptical. Likewise when liberals emphasize anti-corporate measures or Democrats roll out the latest government program. The result of this growing skepticism characterizes the rise of the independents.

A few independents are anti-government and a few are anti-corporation, but the large majority just want government to do its job, do it well, and stop trying to do everything else. While there is heated debate over what, exactly, is the government's job, most independents would settle for good national security, good schools, fiscal responsibility, social equity in the courts, and a high-opportunity economy. While the Left hopes to create a good economy through government programs and the Right through big business initiatives, most independents want both—along with less regulation on small business.

But this tectonic shift in American society is much bigger than politics. Most Americans, and indeed many around the world, have lost faith in modernism itself, in the promise that big, powerful, man-made institutions—be they church, government or corporation—can solve our major problems. Indeed, there is a growing sentiment than most big institutions tend to increase the world's problems.

Business, church and government all have a place in society, the independents say, but none are the "higher" powers we once hoped for.

Postmodernism and Independents

Enter post-modernism. While nearly every person who writes about postmodernism defines it differently, one thing is clear: the fastest growing worldview is not modernism. That is, postmodernists are of many stripes, but they don't believe that government or business will save us. Period.

And they are the new majority.

Independents are likely to read and champion ideas from both Milton Friedman and Ralph Nader, vote for both Barrack Obama and Arnold Schwarzenegger, and quote both Ted Kennedy and Ronald Reagan. Liberals don't understand them, and neither do conservatives.

What is the cause of this social/cultural/political earthquake? At least part of it is that independents no longer have a basic faith in the infallibility or fundamental goodness of either government or the market. They see a role for both, and feel that both must be limited.

The New Majority

But the biggest shift of all may be that postmodernists and independents have a new faith: "We must save ourselves, at least as far as this world is concerned." On one extreme, this means becoming truly self-made, like an Ayn Rand hero, building yourself and your family at the expense of all others.

At another extreme, it includes those who still believe God will save us, but feel that we must live in a way that we deserve to be saved or at least are worthy to live in a God-made world. Most postmodernists adopt neither of these—believing instead that we should become our best selves and help the people around us in the process.

"Humanity needs saving, so do your part," is the growing mantra. If you are in government, do your part and do it well. If you are in business, likewise. Be a great parent, grandparent, doctor, coach, teacher, policeman, nurse, business owner, fireman, mayor, and friend. Whatever your role, do it better.

Some postmodern thinkers, like James Redfield (author of *The Celestine Prophecy)*, promote teams of spiritually-awakened people praying down power from the universe to improve the world. Others, such as intellectual Ken Wilber, suggest learning the truths found in all fields of knowledge and from all cultures and philosophies— and then integrating them together. Mari-anne Williamson says to trust our inner greatness and also in miracles. Many recommend manifesting our personal power to build entrepreneurial wealth and use it to help others.

Nearly every nation and industry has its prophets of manifest-ing success, from Miguel Ruiz and Carlos Castaneda to Anthony Robbins, Brian Tracy, Peter Senge, Ken Blanchard, Paulo Coelho, Guy Kawasaki, Seth Godin or Steve Jobs.

In retrospect, it probably shouldn't surprise anyone that the "self help," "how to," "new age," "success," "skeptic," "green" and "sec-ularist" genres would eventually impact the philosophy of mod-ernism. All of them share a faith in self over institutions. After all, an unproven belief in government or big business is referred to in both "success" and "skeptic" literature as "the victim mentality."

Even atheistic secularism is now turning its back on blind faith in big government and big corporations, replacing it with a "get ahead together" ethic. And the debate between national sover-eignty and globalism is being replaced with the growing concept of *glocalism*—local sovereignty with widespread economic ties.

The Issue Behind the Issues

Where liberals and conservatives talk about things like health care reform, insurance companies and needy patients, indepen-dents talk a lot about living healthier lifestyles, organic foods, and fresh water. They want reform, and they want to make healthier choices in their personal lives as well.

Of course, not all independents are postmodern or "success liter-ature" readers. But few independents now believe that the way to get ahead—personally or nationally—is to turn to government, corporate or other institutional answers.

To say it another way: many independents are postmodernists and don't even know it yet.

Perhaps surprisingly, most independents want to simultaneously:

• succeed economically

• help others

• heal and protect the environment

• keep their nation strong

• build friendlier relationships with other nations

• expand the freedoms of the marketplace

• take care of the needy and the sick

• greatly improve schools

They want government to do its part in this, and corporations too; and they believe that they personally can have a significant positive impact on their little corner of making the world much better.

The media will probably continue to describe the issues in modernist "conservative *versus* liberal" terms. After all, media is a big institution too. But the reality is incredibly powerful: In the 21st century, faith in big institutions is beginning to wane.

Conservatives routinely label independents as "leftists," and liberals call them "right wing." The truth is that most independents are centrists, postmodernists and pragmatists. More to the point, while almost everyone else is pointing fingers or turning to government or corporations for leadership, independents are quietly and consistently increasing their personal education, holdings and influence.

How to See What is Really Happening

It remains to be seen how all this will play out, but for years to come the real issue behind the issues will be the rising power of independents, most of whom do not have much faith in big institutions. When independents side with a government program, liberals will claim they won the support of the American people. When independents prefer a market approach, conservatives will claim victory. In reality, however, winning policies will be those that gain the support of independents.

If you want to know the future of any issue, find out how independents view it. And if it appears that a big-institution issue is winning, find out why independents support it; they usually support a certain reform, not the institution behind the reform.

Through all the politics and media reports, if current trends continue, faith in and deep support for big institutions will slowly dwindle. It is unclear exactly what will replace it, but that replacement may well be the biggest story of the 21st Century.

"Mr. Head Democrat" (or Republican)

In my book *The Coming Aristocracy,* I wrote that the United States now lives in the era of the permanent campaign. A young pollster in the Carter administration by the name of Patrick Caddell coined the term back in 1976, and he hit the nail right on the head. America used to gear up for campaigns, elect one of the candidates, and then settle down to let the winner lead the nation.

Not anymore. Now we elect a candidate and then immediately increase the fervor of the debate. We pick sides before an election, and once the election is over we get really serious about the fight.

In the modern era of politics since Watergate, this permanent battle trend has continually increased. It is a new kind of politics, where few things are about leadership or wisdom and everything is about beating the other side.

In the 2008 presidential campaign, I expected Senator Clinton to win the election—and I was surprised when Barrack Obama took the Democratic nomination. I quickly set out to learn everything I could about him, from original sources—his writings, speeches and public utterances.

What I found was interesting: Obama's pre-presidential record and especially his book, *The Audacity of Hope,* was a blend of charismatic-populist leadership with old-line liberal politics. The Democratic Party hadn't seen that alchemical mixture since JFK.

My prediction was that Obama's populism would bring him a victory and then we'd see whether he emphasized leadership or liberalism. If he emphasized the leadership aspect, I said, he would become one of the great presidents of American history. It was Leader Obama *versus* Politician Obama, and I was very interested to see which one would win out in the realities of modern Washington.

Three Americas

If you watched the historic election night 2008 and listened to the now-famous "Yes We Can" speech, perhaps you already share my opinion that this was the height of Leader Obama. Leader Obama did something truly amazing for a Democrat in the modern political era—he carried a majority of the wealthy voters (those who make over $200,000 per year). He was the first Democrat to do so in the post-Watergate era, and this amazing statistic seemed to indicate a new type of politics ahead. But Politician Obama's hard shift to the left after inauguration changed this dynamic.

Note that the change wasn't among conservatives—they never liked him and few voted for him. The shift was in the 39% of the voting population that didn't want to be called either liberals or conservatives.

This tri-lateral divide of the American political landscape is fascinating. There are roughly 28% of us who would donate to the Sierra Club, a competing 28% who would donate to The National Rifle Association, and a whopping 39% made up of two kinds of people: those who would donate to neither, and those who would donate to both!

We have the liberals in one camp, the conservatives in another, and in the largest faction we find a mixed bag called independents. The far left and extreme right form their own small camps at the fringes.

"Mr. Head Democrat"

When President Obama took office he had a 70% approval rating—liberals, most of the far left, and nearly all of the independents. By September 1, 2009 his approval rating was down to 50%. This is the biggest fall in the history of new presidents in so short a time, as David Brooks wrote in *The New York Times*.[52] And the rating would continue to decline.

In less than eight months after his inauguration, President Obama was seen by most Americans less as President of the United States and more as the Head Democrat. Politician over Leader.

This was the same story in the Bush Administration. Conservatives saw him as the President and liberals as the Head Republican. The Clinton presidency experienced the same pattern. This split of the parties is normal and expected.

But the telling point is how independents see Presidents. When they see a president as leader, popularity and support soars; the opposite occurs when independents see a president as politician.

Independent Power

The power resides in the independents, though neither major party has yet to fully embrace this truth. Independents want three main things: sound fiscal policy, strong national defense, and the decentralization of power (including preservation of state, local and individual powers). Independents are more pragmatic than ideological; they don't engage in emotional party-supporting, and they just want things to work.

Independents want to be safe from international and terrorist attacks, free, and prosperous. They want a strong government that does certain things very well and leaves the rest to the state, local or private sectors.

When the Bush Administration started its tenure with these goals, it won the conservative and independent votes and support, but lost independents when it turned to big government answers and huge spending increases (much higher than Clinton Administration budgets).

When Leader Obama promised to cut foreign spending and bring a new era of real leadership to Washington, independents supported his candidacy against the daunting possibility of continued Bush-like policies under McCain.

This trend is just getting started. Independents are also withdrawing their support from Congress any time they watch it turn to party politics and shun leadership.

Of course, many liberals still consider Democratic Presidents great leaders, just as many conservatives support Republican Presidents even when they make glaring mistakes and try to spend and regulate their way to popularity. But independents aren't tied to any one party. They want results, and they'll support candidates, Presidents and other officials who get the results they seek.

In this environment, leadership means getting support for your projects from your own party *plus independents*. Anything else fails.

Three long-term issues drive presidential politics in the U.S.: national security, the economy, and a sense of leadership. Win two, and you win the presidency. Win three, like the Republicans did with Reagan and the Democrats with Obama, and you win the Congress too.

A Tipping Point Trend

This rise of the independents is creating an interesting tension between the two-party system and the voting electorate. For too long the two parties held a virtual monopoly on American politics, and the citizens had to pick a side or lose all influence. As a result, most Americans stopped being actively involved in government issues. But with the rise of the Internet and independents, more and more regular citizens are getting deeply involved.

The power of the independents will increase the divide between the left and the right. Indeed, an era of shifting like the one we are experiencing is marked by such divisions. The first two such shifts in American history created a new political party—the Democratic Republicans in 1798 and later the Republicans in 1856.

The last time we faced such a major shift we totally restructured government power by creating the Social Security Administration, the United Nations, the World Bank, The International Monetary Fund, a host of secretive agencies in Washington, and a drastic increase in government regulations and red tape.

Whatever the current shift brings, let's hope for more of a Freedom*Shift* than a transfer of more power to Washington. Some may say that a rebirth of freedom is too hard, that we can't do it. Our response should be, "Yes, we can!" In truth, it is a matter of leadership over politics.

If independents keep being stifled in both of the major parties, their frustration will continue to grow. When they side with the Democrats, the result is usually more spending on national programs that further undermine America's fiscal strength, free-market system, and national defense. When they side with Republicans, the result has been increased spending on international projects and even corrupt governance that weakens the economy, freedoms and American power.

In short, at some point independents are likely to either totally reform one of the parties or just start their own.

Investing in the Future

On a personal level, many independents invest in gold (which always seems to increase in value when the government spends beyond its means) and McDonalds (which grows when the economy is booming and keeps growing internationally even when the U.S. economy recedes).[53]

On a national level, during a time of shifting it is natural to see people a little confused about where they stand. After all, the constants they have believed probably don't apply anymore. For example, Republicans are no longer the party of the rich and Democrats have quit being the party of the little guy.

Also, voters can no longer count on the old certainties that Republicans want to reduce the size of government and Democrats want to decrease foreign involvements and focus on domestic policy. Indeed, now both Republicans and Democrats drastically increase government spending and foreign entanglements—whoever is in office.

Learning From Both Sides

I once invited a regional well-known liberal and vocal Democrat to speak at a graduation ceremony for George Wythe University. His speech was liberal and, well—*liberal*. Afterwards a number of conservatives railed and argued for days about our selection of speaker. The students, in contrast, learned a great deal and the speech provided material for many long discussions and assignments.

A few liberals congratulated me on our selection of speaker, but a number of conservatives called with their frustration. A few donors even stopped sending contributions. A few years later we invited a conservative talk-show host to speak at a gala event, and the entire process repeated itself; only this time the conservatives were happy, the liberals were upset, and once again the students and anyone willing to relax and listen learned a great deal.

The most intriguing lessons from both of these events came from the few who made a point of really listening and learning from views not naturally their own. We often learn more in our disagreements than from those who just repeat what we already "know."

Nearly all who closely listened and learned from the speaker of a differing viewpoint exhibited the basic views of independents. This is a rising power in America, as of yet largely unnoticed, but sure to shift everything in the years ahead.

Winning Elections and Hearts Through Leadership

I doubt that any U.S. President, liberal or conservative, will be seen by the nation any time soon as truly "Mr. President" rather than "Mr. Head Democrat /or/ Republican." When it does happen, it will be because of a war or a Mister or Madam President who drops partisan politics and adopts the values of independents: strong national defense, a free economic system that spurs prosperity, and a strong and active government that does what it should and also leaves the rest to state, local and private entities.

I look forward to being led by such a President, current or future, whose policies win the long-term support of Party + Independents. That's leadership. Anything else is merely partisan politics. In every election for the next few decades at least, the biggest block of voting Americans will go searching for a leader who will finally represent their goals. Whatever happens in elections, this growing group is poised to remake the future of American politics.

A Tale of Two Parties

The emerging and improving technologies of the Information Age have reinvented government by forcing leaders to constantly serve two masters: governance and politics. Governance is a process of details and nuance, but politics is more about symbols than substance.

As I stated in *The Coming Aristocracy*, before the past two decades politics were the domain of elections, which had a compact and intense timeline. After elections, officials had a period to focus on governing, and then a short time before the subsequent elections they would return to politics during the campaign period. Now, however, governors, legislators and presidential administrations are required to fight daily, year-round, on both these fronts.

Both major parties struggle in this new structure. Those in power must dedicate precious time and resources to politics instead of leadership. Worst of all, decisions that used to be determined at least some of the time by actual governance policy are now heavily influenced by political consideration—almost without exception.

The Loyal Opposition

The party out of power has less of a challenge, but even it is expected to present alternate governance plans for nearly every-thing—plans which have no chance of ever being adopted, and are therefore a monumental misuse of official time and energy—instead of focusing on their vital role of loyal opposition which should ensure weighty and principled consideration of national priorities.

The temptation to politicize this process is nearly overwhelming—meaning that the opposition party has basically abandoned any aspiration or intent to participate in the process of governing and has become all-politics, all-the-time.

As a result, American leadership from both parties is weakened.

With the advancement of technology in recent years has come the increased facility for individuals to not only access news and information in real time, but to participate in the dialog by generating commentary, drawing others' attention to under-reported issues and ideas, and influencing policy through blogging, online discussions and grass-roots campaigns. An immensely important consequence of this technological progress has been the fractionalizing of the parties.

Civics 102a

High school civics classes for the past century have taught that America had a two-party system. And up until the end of the Cold War, this was actually true. Each party had clear, distinct values and goals, and voters had simply to assess the differences and choose which to support.

Such clarity is long gone today, and there is no evidence that this will change any time soon. As a result, more people now call themselves "independents" than either "Democrats" or "Republicans."

We are led today by the contests and relations of seven competing factions, or parties. These major factions are as follows:

Republicans

1. Nixonians

2. Reaganites

3. Populists

Democrats

4. Leftists

5. Pragamatists

6. Special Interests

Either/Neither

7. Independents

Neither party knows what to do about this. Both are plagued by deep divisions. When a party wins the White House, these divisions are largely ignored. During a party's time in the White House, the underpinnings of the party weaken as differences are downplayed and disaffection quietly grows. Fewer people wanted to be identified as Republicans with each passing year under the Bush administration, just as the Democratic coalition weakened during the Clinton years.

This is a trend with no recent exceptions. Being the party in power actually tends to weaken popular support over time. Power facilitates governance, but reduces political strength. Every governance policy tends to upset at least a few supporters, who now look elsewhere for "better" leadership.

While Republicans and Democrats accomplish it in slightly different ways, both alienate supporters as they use their power once elected. We are led today by the contests and relations of seven competing factions, or parties. Let's learn a little about each of them and how they influence our freedoms.

Republicans: The Party of Nixon *versus* The Party of Reagan

Both Nixon and Reagan were nominal Republicans; but symbolically they are nearly polar opposites of all but the staunchest Republican loyalists.

Today's Reaganites value:

• strong national security and schools

- fiscal responsibility
- laws which incentivize small businesses and entrepreneurial enterprises

Nixonians (who, for some reason, don't the use this label) value:
- party loyalty over ideology
- government policy that benefits big business and large corporations
- international interventionism
- winning elections

A third faction in the Republican community are the populists. Feeling disenfranchised by the loss of the Party to the Nixonians, the populists want Americans to "wake up," realize that "everything is going socialist," and "take back our nation."

Identified with and defined by the shrill voices and divisive rhetoric of talk-show figureheads, the populists are seen as more *against* than *for* anything. They believe that government is simply too big, and that anything which shrinks or stalls government is patently good.

A Bad Day To Be A Populist

The populists are doomed to perpetual disappointment since any time they win an election they watch their candidate "sell out." It is hard to imagine a more thankless job than that of the candidate elected by populist vote. Once she takes office she is consigned to offend and alienate either her constituents or her colleagues—most likely both. She is either completely ineffective at achieving the goals of her constituency, or, if she learns to function within the machine, she has no constituency left.

Any candidate who tries to work within the system will lose her appeal to the populists. If such a candidate stays focused on principle, like the iconic Ron Paul, populists will admire his purity but will criticize his lack of substantive impact—his accomplishments are seen as almost exclusively symbolic.

Some of the most influential populist pundits (like Rush Limbaugh) have lost "believers" by being outspokenly populist when they support the party agenda (like during the Clinton Administration and later in rejecting McCain's presidential candidacy as too moderate and even liberal) and then switching to support the Party (backing President Bush even in liberal policies and supporting McCain when he became the Republican nominee). This is seen by detractors as manipulative, corrupt and Nixonian at worst, and self-serving, hypocritical and opportunist at best.

Vast Right Wing Conspiracy

Populism is considered "crazy" by most intellectuals in the media and elsewhere. This is probably inevitable and unchangeable given that the same things that appeal popularly (such as alarmism, extremism, labeling, using symbols, images, hyperbole and appeals to sentimentalism) are considered anti-truth to intellectuals. Indeed, part of training the intellect in the Western tradition is to reject the message of such deliveries without serious consideration, and dismiss the messenger as either unfit or unworthy to have a serious debate on issues.

Wise intellectuals look past the delivery and consider the actual message. This being said, even when weighed on its own merit the populist message is unpopular with intellectuals. Populism is based on the assumption that the gut feelings of the masses (The Wisdom of Crowds) are a better source of wisdom than the considered charts, graphs and analysis by teams of experts. This hits a little too close to home for those who make their living in academia, the media or government. So our system seems naturally to pit the will of the people against the wisdom of the few.

Crazy Like A Fox

It is interesting to compare and contrast this modern debate between the wisdom of the populists and that of experts and officials with the American founding view. The brilliance of the founders was their tendency to correctly characterize the tendencies of a group in society and employ that nature to its best use in the grand design in order to perpetuate freedom and prosperity.

In fact, the American framers did empower the masses to make certain vital decisions—called *elections*. Madison rightly called every election a peaceful revolution.

And, the founders did empower small groups of experts: the framers had senators, judges, ambassadors, the president and his ministers appointed by teams of experts. Only the House of Representatives and various state and local officials were elected by the masses, and the House alone was given power over the money and how it was spent.

In short: The founders thought that the masses would best determine two things:

• Who should make the nation's money decisions

• Who should appoint our other leaders

Riddle: When Is A Democracy Not A Democracy?

The founders believed that most of the nation's governance should come from competing teams of experts, as long as the masses got to decide who would appoint those experts and how much money they could spend.

Such a system naturally empowers and employs both populism and expertise.

If It Ain't Broke, Don't Fix It

Compare today's model: Senators are now elected by the populace and the electoral college has been weakened so that the popular vote has much more impact on electing a president than it once did (and than the founders intended), thus increasing the power of the popular vote. Yet many of the same "intellectuals" who support ending the Electoral College altogether ironically consider populists "crazy" and "extremist." The incongruity is extreme.

The reason for this seeming paradox is simple: Where the founding era actually believed in the wisdom of the populace to elect, modern intellectuals seem to believe that few of these "crazies" actually believe what they say they believe. Many intellectuals think that populists, conservatives and most of the masses are simply following the views provided by talking heads.

But at its core, the alarmist and wild antics of populist pundits are not the real reason many intellectuals question the sanity of conservative populists. The deeper reason is that few intellectuals believe that *sane people don't want more government*. They understand Nixonian Republicans and their desire for more power, government support of Big Business and less regulation of corporations.

They may not agree with these goals, but they don't defy their comprehension. They also understand poor and middle class citizens wanting more government help. And they even understand the Reaganesque vision of fiscal responsibility along with strong schools, security and increased incentives for small business.

Does No Mean Yes?

What intellectuals struggle to understand are lower and middle class voters who don't want government programs. For example, in their view, few of the populist "crazies" who opposed President Obama's healthcare would be taxed to pay for it, and most would see their family's health care benefits increased by Democratic plans. So why would they—*how could they*—oppose it? *Rich right-wing leaders who would bear the costs for health care must have convinced them.*

This is a logical (but inaccurate) conclusion. Rich people opposing higher taxes makes sense. Lower and middle class people supporting increased government aide makes sense. Rich talk show hosts telling people Democratic plans are bad makes sense. The people being duped by this makes sense.

What *doesn't* make sense to many, what few intellectuals are willing to accept, is that large numbers of non-intellectuals are looking past alarmist talk show host antics, closely studying the issues and deciding to choose the principles of limited government over direct, personal, monetary benefit.

Intellectuals could respect such a choice: lots of citizens refusing government benefits to help the nation's economy and freedom would be an amazing, selfless act of patriotism. But they can't bring themselves to believe this is happening. Instead, they are concerned that the "wing nuts" are following extremist pundits and unknowingly refusing personal benefit. That's "crazy!" This view is reinforced by the non-intellectual and often wild-eyed way some populists behave, and the way they talk about the issues.

In this same vein, intellectuals also naturally support the end of the Electoral College because it would naturally give them, especially the media, even more political influence. The most frustrating thing for intellectuals is this: The possibility that these "crazies" aren't really crazy at all—that they actually see the biased focus and struggle for power by the intellectual media and don't want to be duped by it. Such a segment of society naturally diminishes the potential influence of the media, and is treated by many as a threat.

By the way, many conservative populists claim to be Reaganites. In fairness, they do align with a major Reagan tenet—an anti-incumbent, anti-Washington, anti-insider, anti-government attitude. These were central *Candidate* Reagan themes. However, once in office, *President* Reagan governed with big spending for security, schools and the other Reaganite objectives listed earlier. This is a typical Republican pattern. For example, compare the second Bush Administration's election attacks on Clinton's spending with the reality of Bush's huge budget increases—far above Clintonian levels.

Democrats: Leftists, Leaders and Special Interests

Having covered the Republican divisions, the discussion of the Democratic Party will be simpler. The three major factions are similar: those seeking power, those wanting to promote liberal ideas, and the extreme fringe. Let's start with the fringe.

Where Republican "fringies" call for the large-scale reduction of government, Democratic extremists want government to fund, fix, regulate and get deeply involved in specific special interests. And while conservative populists are generally united in wanting government to be reduced across the board, Democratic special interests are many, and in constant competition with each other for precious government funds and public awareness.

While Republican extremists see the government, Democrats and "socialists" as the enemy, Democratic radicals see corporations, big business, Republicans and the House of Representatives (regardless of who is in power) as enemies.

Republican "crazies" distrust a Democratic White House, the FBI, Hollywood, the Federal Reserve, Europe, the media and the Supreme Court. Democrat "crazies" hate Republican presidents, the CIA, Wall Street, Rush Limbaugh, hick towns, gun manufacturers, Fox News and evangelical activists. Republican extremists like talk show hosts and Democratic extremists like trial lawyers.

How's that for stereotyping?

A Rainbow Fringe

The Republican populist group is one faction—the anti-government faction. Radical Democrats are a conglomerate of many groups—from "-isms" like feminism and environmentalism to ethnic empowerment groups and dozens of other special interests, large and small, seeking the increased support and advocacy of government.

One thing Democrat extremists generally agree on is that the rich and especially the super-rich must be convinced to solve most of the world's problems. Ralph Nader, for example, argues that this must be done using the power of the super-rich to do what government hasn't been able to accomplish: drastically reduce the power of big corporations.

No matter which party currently holds the White House, the extreme factions have a lot less influence within the party than did, say, the –ism fringes during the Bush years—or than Republican extremists did under Obama. The call for a "big tent" is a temporary utilitarian tactic to gain and conglomerate power when a party is in the minority. When a party is in power, its two big factions run the show.

Call the two largest Democratic factions the "Governance" faction and the "Politics" faction.

For Democrats, the Politics faction is interested in:

- maintaining national security while trying to reroute resources from defense to other priorities
- increasing the popularity of the U.S. in the eyes of the world and especially Europe
- promoting a general sense of increasing social justice, racial and gender equality, improved environmental and energy policy
- improving the economy through government spending

A major weakness of this faction is its tendency toward elitism and self-righteous arrogance.

Is That Too Much To Ask?

The Governance faction has to do something nobody else—not the other Democrat factions, not the Republican factions, and certainly not the independents—is required to accomplish. It is expected to bring to pass the following:

• Keep America safe from foreign and terrorist attacks

• Pass laws which institutionalize the liberal agenda

• Keep the economy from tanking

• Improve the economic statistics of the nation

When the Democratic Governance faction accomplishes these four, it achieves both its short-term governance *and* its political goals. If it fails in any of them, it inevitably loses much of its independent support.

When Democrats create scandals like Clinton's handling of his affairs or overreach as in the Obama Administration's "war on Fox News," independents see them as Nixonian and respond by distancing themselves both philosophically and in the voting booth.

When it comes to elections, independents are powerfully swayed by "The Leadership Thing," and Obama, Clinton and Reagan clearly had it—but not Bush, Dole, Bush, Gore, Kerry or McCain.

But "The Leadership Thing" runs in candidates only—not in parties, and, apparently, not in presidents.

Obama won because so many independents supported him. Independents are a separate faction—one that truly belongs to neither party.

The danger of the two-party monopoly is extreme. Even U.S. Presidents can't seem to crack it. For example, President Bush was labeled a liar about Weapons of Mass Destruction (WMD's) in Iraq by such Democratic Leaders as Ted Kennedy, John Kerry, John Edwards and Hillary Clinton, even though every single one of these people gave speeches themselves saying that Iraq had WMD's. They also claimed to have reviewed the intelligence themselves.

Let me repeat that: Shortly after 9/11 the Bush Administration and top Senators from both parties reviewed the available intelligence and told the American people that Saddam Hussein had WMD's. Later, when the Democratic leaders turned on President Bush for following up on this intelligence, the American people blamed Republicans for the "lie." But the Democratic leaders didn't just claim that Bush had lied to them, they claimed to have reviewed the intelligence themselves. And, in fact, the Clinton Administration claimed that Iraq had WMD's before Bush even ran for President.

I don't know if Iraq had any WMD's or not, whether they were sent to Syria like some suggested or not, or whether the intelligence was just plain wrong like the media now report. But when the leaders of both parties claimed that there were WMD's, we should blame both parties if it turns out to be untrue.

The problem is listening too much to either party. They both want to win elections, so they spin everything with the elections in mind. Studying both parties and other non-partisan views is vital for free citizens. Republicans should study both the Governing and Political factions of the Democratic Party, not to find quotes to attack, but rather to find proposals worth supporting as well as those that need to be opposed. Democrats should do the same with Republican factions.

Unfortunately, the party spoils system makes this unlikely. Which is exactly why independents now are the swing voters. Independents study the proposals and ideas of both parties and other views, looking for things that will work and supporting them and also rejecting things they find objectionable.

Capturing the Middle Ground

Without the support of independents, none of these groups from either party can get their way. Unfortunately for the two monopoly parties, and thankfully for the nation, independents are actively involved in watching the symbols of governance as well as studying the details of policy. They are not easily impressed or swayed. They are more like the citizens of the American founding than any generation since before the Great Depression.

Who are these people that vacillate between the parties? Are they wishy-washy, never-satisfied uber-idealist pessimists? Are they the weakest among us? Are they ignorant, poor or backward? Are they dangerous? Why don't they just pick a party and show some loyalty, some commitment, like Steelers fans or staunch religionists?

Actually, independents are the most consistent voters in America. True, they fluctuate between parties and seldom cast a straight party ballot, but they vote for the same things in nearly all elections. In contrast, party loyalists stick with their party even when it adopts policies they patently disagree with. Some might argue that while this does show commitment to party, it is a pretty "wishy-washy" way to approach citizenship and voting.

Independents watch the issues, candidates and government officials very closely, since they don't rely on party platforms or personalities to define their values, or to recommend affiliations on which to bestow their trust.

What They Want

Independents want strong national security, open and effective diplomacy, good schools, policies that benefit small businesses and families, social/racial/gender equality, and just, effective and efficient law enforcement. They see a positive role for government in all these, and dislike the right-wing claim that any government involvement in these issues is socialistic. As noted previously: Taxing the middle class to bail out the upper and upper-middle class (bankers, auto-makers, etc.) is not socialism; it's aristocracy.

Independents are unconvinced by Republican arguments that government should give special benefits to large corporations, or Democratic desires to involve government in many arenas beyond the basics. Independents care about the environment, privacy, parental rights, reducing racial and religious bigotry, and improving government policy on immigration and other issues.

A Tough Sell

On three big issues—healthcare, taxation and boosting the economy—independents side with neither Democrats nor Republicans. They want good health care laws, taxes and economic policies that favor neither Wall Street corporations (Republican model) nor Washington regulators (Democratic model). They want the policies designed to benefit small businesses and families in order to spur increased prosperity.

Independents want government to be strong and effective in serving society in ways best suited to the state, but they expect it to do so wisely and with fiscal responsibility.

They tend to see Republicans as over-spenders on international interventions that fail to improve America's security, and Democrats as wasteful on domestic programs that fail to deliver desired outcomes.

They want government to spend money on programs that work and truly improve the nation and the world. They are often seen as moderates because they reject both the right-wing argument against constructive and effective government action and leftist faith in more government programs regardless of results. They want to cut programs that don't work, support the ones that do, and adopt additional initiatives that show promise and provide accountability for results.

American Independents and American Independence

The future of America, and American independence, will likely be determined by independents. Interestingly, independents come from all six of the other factions mentioned in this chapter.

The one thing they nearly all have in common is that they usually don't see themselves as part of a specific party, but rather as independent citizens and voters. And they are more actively involved in studying and influencing government than citizens have been for many decades.

The technologies of the past twenty years have made things more difficult for politicians, but they have made it easier for citizens to stand up for freedom. What we do with this increase in our potential power remains to be seen.

CHAPTER

12

The New Global Elite Class

In a two-day span, *The New York Times* ran two articles—"The Tel Aviv Cluster" and "Is China the Next Enron?"—on the strengths and weaknesses of China and Israel. Written by Thomas Friedman and David Brooks, the articles arrived at surprisingly similar conclusions.

First, at the time of the articles, both nations were economic hotspots, primarily because of the high numbers of entrepreneurs within each. Where America has become a capitol of employeeship, in Israel and China the American Dream of "making it" through business initiative and entrepreneurial enterprise is alive and well. India could certainly be included in this.

Second, both are zones of technological growth. Of course, this stems from entrepreneurial innovation. Where the U.S. trains most of the world's attorneys, Chinese, Israeli and Indian students dominate engineering and technology enrollments in many of the world's leading schools.

Third, China, Israel and India appear to be on the verge of major shifts. The Chinese challenge ahead is to bring its political institutions up to speed with the rapid spread of economic liberties. The Soviet Union collapsed because it tried to reform by expanding political liberty while maintaining a command economy. Traditional Chinese communism also rejected freedom at all levels, and the attempt now is to offer economic freedom while keeping a totalitarian government.

The huge amount of savings, including "$2 trillion in foreign currency revenues"[54] available to the Chinese government gives it a lot of power into the future. What kind of volatility is ahead for a nation with an authoritarian and oppressive government that also has the world's largest entrepreneurial class?

As for Israel, the challenge is that increased economic and technological successes further widen the gap between Israel and its already estranged neighbors. This is a huge destabilizing factor. As Brooks says, "Israel is an astonishing success story, but also a highly mobile one." He suggests that if the region destabilizes, the entrepreneurial class already has connections and homes in Palo Alto, for example.[55]

As for India, it is still plagued by a static class system that largely determines one's access to opportunities from education to business start-up capital. In response, it is finding ways to treat foreign capital extremely well in order to lure international entrepreneurs. This strategy is proving successful here and also in several nations in Latin America, Oceana and Asia.

American Decline

Perhaps the most telling message of these articles is the contrast with the United States. We're cutting technology programs and increasing the regulatory, tax and red-tape obstacles for entrepreneurs. Positive gains in U.S. social justice since 1964 have unfortunately and unnecessarily coincided with the dismantling of American incentives for entrepreneurial free enterprise. Current levels of U.S. business regulations don't allow many American entrepreneurs to effectively compete with their international competitors.

Trends in China, India, Israel and elsewhere provide more evidence for one of the most important developments in our world: The rise of a new global elite class. Interestingly, Friedman and Brooks have both written books about this new elite.[56]

For example, Friedman introduced the concept of the Electronic

Herd, a new, highly mobile elite class that manages the world's capital from their laptops and lives in places like Mediterranean beach towns on the Spanish or French Riviera, Ashland (Oregon), Austin (Texas), the Bahamas, Buenos Aires, London and so on. This group parties in Manhattan and Switzerland, reads both the great classics of humanity and today's financials, and has little connection with or allegiance to the government of any nation.

Rediscovering the American Dream

America became known around the world for two great ideals: 1) freedom, and 2) a classless society where anybody could become whatever they were willing to earn and achieve. Together we often called these ideals The American Dream. As the U.S. regulated away our free enterprise strategic advantage—especially since 1989— its cities become more and more like the class-based European models that many American cultural elites idealize.

Today, America's "aristocrats" are likely to be less loyal to the United States than to their corporate connections, and many Americans who consider themselves patriots are too likely to be dependent on job wages and living paycheck to paycheck. Canada and various other nations are in the same situation. The irony here is thick.

Those who care most about freedom (many of whom are independents) may have more to learn from examples like Israel, China and India than from contemporary Washington D.C. and its increasingly Europeanized institutions, dreams and objectives.

The Effectiveness of Liberty

Just like during the American founding era, freedom in our day will flourish again in any place emphasizing entrepreneurship, free enterprise initiative and major deregulation of small business and class-oriented structures. Where many nations can learn from America's current example of social justice, the U.S.

needs a healthy renaissance of economic and political freedom.

Until our leaders, institutions and laws once again lead the world in allowing and incentivizing entrepreneurial initiative, our freedoms and prosperity will decrease. It is time for America to import its most valuable resource: A widespread belief in free enterprise.

The world needs less of a growing elite class and more nations where freedom is adopted and applied. Independents are on the cutting edge of this shift.

chapter 13

The Latch Key Generation and Independents

The rise of independents isn't an accident. It is the natural result of both major parties emphasizing politics over principle, and ideology over pragmatism.

Another reason for the rise of independents is the widespread loss of faith in man-made institutions (like government and corporations) as the answers to society's challenges. These institutions have failed to perform, over and over, causing many of even the staunchest state- and market-loyalists to feel skeptical.

Also, the *e*-revolution has created a technological power of the citizenry, at least in the ability to widely voice views that diverge from the mainstream parties. The Internet gave independents (and many others) a voice. People who believed in common-sense pragmatism and principled choices over party loyalty have been around for a long time; but the *e*-revolution was needed to give them tribe influence.

But all of these reasons are really just after-the-fact justifications for why so many people are no longer channeled politically through one of the top parties. They explain why people aren't Republicans or Democrats, but they don't explain why independents are independents.

Some independents are actually from the far right and just anti-liberal, and others are leftists who are independents because they are anti-conservative. Some are one-issue independents, emphasizing the environment, feminism, race relations, the gold standard, etc.

A growing number of independents, however, are independents because they believe in a shared new ideal. They have faith in both government and the market, but only to a certain extent. They are truly neither liberal nor conservative, but moderate. They want government and markets to work, and they want to limit both as needed. Still, they are not just moderates; they are something more.

Three Versions of Management

What makes the majority of independents tick? They are motivated by a new focus, a set of goals surprising and even confusing to anyone who was taught that American politics is about right *versus* left, conservative *versus* liberal, family values *versus* progressivism, religious *versus* secular, hawk *versus* dove, and all the other clichés.

Independents are something new.

Former Gore speechwriter Daniel Pink argues that business is going through a major shift, that the entire landscape of incentives for employees, executives and even owner-investors is changing. Our ancestors were motivated mostly by "Management 1.0," Pink says, which was a focus on physical safety and protection from threats.

"Management 2.0" came when people learned to produce things in a routine way, from planned agriculture to assembly-line industry. People became more motivated by a "carrot and stick" model of "extrinsic motivators." Managers, teachers, parents and politicians created complex systems of rewards and punishments, penalties and bonuses to achieve results in this new environment.

In this model, conservatives are 1.0 because they want government to limit itself to protecting its citizens from external threats, to national security and legal justice. Liberals support a 2.0 model where the role of government is to incentivize positive community behaviors by people and organizations, and also to enforce a complex system of punishments to deter negative behavior. This doesn't mean that 2.0 is better or even more advanced than 1.0, but it is certainly a different viewpoint, and tends to gain traction in the current psycho-social climate.

In education, 1.0 is the one-room schoolhouse focusing on delivering a quality, personalized education for each student. In contrast, 2.0 is a conveyor-belt system that socializes all students and provides career rewards through job training, with benefits doled out based on academic and social performance.

The problem with 1.0 is that education is withheld from some based on race, wealth and sometimes gender or religion. The 2.0 version remedies this, ostensibly providing democratic equality for students from all backgrounds; but the cost is that personalization and quality are lost, and a de facto *new* elite class is created by those who succeed in this educational matrix.

On the political plane, 1.0 promoted freedom but only for an elite few, while 2.0 emphasized social justice, but out of pragmatism it unnecessarily sacrificed many freedoms. Version 3.0 combines freedom with inclusion, and this is the basis of the new independents and their ideals.

Management 3.0

It may seem oxymoronic to say that pragmatic independents have ideals, but they are actually as driven as conservatives and liberals. Independents want government, markets and society to work, and to work well. They don't believe in utopia, but they do think that government has an important role (along with business), and that many other individuals and organizations have vital roles in making society work. They aren't seeking perfect society, but they do think there is a common sense way in which the world can generally work a lot better than it does.

Mr. Pink's "Management 3.0" is a widespread cultural shift toward "intrinsic motivators." A growing number of people today (according to Pink) are making decisions based less on the fear of threats (1.0), or to avoid punishments or obtain rewards (2.0), than on following their hearts (3.0).

This isn't "right-brained" idealism or abstraction, but logic-based, rational and often self-centered attempts to seek one's most likely path to happiness. Indeed, disdain for the "secure career path" has become widely engrained in our collective mentality and is associated with being shallow, losing one's way, and ignoring your true purpose and self.

This mindset is now our *culture*. For example, watch a contemporary movie or television series; the plot is either 1.0 (catch or kill the bad guys) or 3.0 (struggle to fit in to the 2.0 system but overcome it by finding one's unique true path). Settling for mediocrity in order to fit the system is today's frustrated view of 2.0. In contrast, the two main versions of 3.0 movies are: 1) Ayn Rand-style characters seeking personal fulfillment, and 2) Gene Rodenberry-style heroes who "find themselves" in order to greatly benefit the happiness of all.

Where the Greeks had tragedy or comedy, our generation either finds itself for personal gain or to improve the world—preferably both. Whichever version we choose, the key is to truly find and live our life purpose and be who we were meant to be. And where this has so far grown and taken hold in our pop-culture and generational mindset, it is now poised to impact politics. It may well be that few of the old guard in media, academia or government realize how powerful this trend is.

Generations

Independents are the latchkey generation grown up. Raised by themselves, with input from peers, they are skeptical of parents' (conservative) overtures of care after years of emotional distance. They are unmoved by parents' (liberal) emotional insecurity and constant but unfulfilled promises. They don't trust television, experts or academics.

They don't get too connected to any current view on an issue; they know that however passionate they may feel about it right now, relationships come and go like the latest technology and the only one you can always count on is yourself. Because of this, you must do what you love in life and make a good living doing it. This isn't abstract or even idealistic; it's hard-core realism.

Loyalty to political party makes no sense to two generations forced to realize very young the limitations of their parents, teachers and other adults. Why would such a generation give any kind of implicit trust to government, corporations, political parties or other "adult" figures?

Independents are more swayed by Google, Amazon and Whole Foods than Hollywood, Silicon Valley or Yale. Appeals to authority such as the Congressional Budget Office, the United Nations or Nobel Prize winners mean little to them; they'll study the issues themselves. They read voraciously, consider, debate and trust their own views more than the agendas of experts.

Their view of the experts is that whatever the outside world thinks of them, they are most likely far too human at home. Officials and experts with noteworthy accolades, lofty credentials and publicized achievements make independents more skeptical than star-struck. They grew up with distant and distracted "corporate stars" for parents, and they aren't impressed.

Having moved around throughout their formative years, never allowed to put down deep roots in any one town or school for long, why would they feel a powerful connection to country or nation? If the government follows good principles, they'll support it. If not, they'll look elsewhere. They understand being disappointed and having to move on and rely on themselves; in fact, this is so fundamental to their makeup that it is almost an unconscious religion.

If this all sounds too negative, consider the positives. The American founding had many similar generational themes. Raised mostly by domestic help (parents were busy overcoming many out-of-the-home challenges in this generation), sent away to boarding schools or apprenticeships before puberty, the founders learned loyalty to principles over traditions, pragmatic common sense over the assurances of experts, and an idealistic yearning for improving the world over contentment with the current.

Today's independents represent one of the most founders-like generations since the 1770s. They want the world to change, they want it to work, and they depend on themselves and peers rather than "adults" (experts, officials, etc.) to make it happen.

Independent Philosophy

There are many reasons independents don't resonate with the two major parties; but this is only part of the story. Most independents aren't just disenfranchised liberals or conservatives, they are a new generation with entirely new goals and views on government, business and society.

This is all hidden to most, because the latchkey generation isn't as expressive or emotive as most liberals and conservatives. Trained to keep things inside, not to confide in their parents or adults, growing numbers of independents are nonetheless quietly and surely increasing their power, worth and influence.

Few independents believe that there will be any Social Security monies left for them when they retire, so they are stoically planning to take care of themselves. Still, they think government should pay up on its promise to take care of the Boomers, and they are willing to pay their part. Indeed, this basically sums up their entire political philosophy: *Government should do its part, and so should the rest of us. But as for me: I'll make my own arrangements.*

Most independents disdain the political debate that so vocally animates liberals and conservatives, and as a result they have little voice in the traditional media because they refuse to waste time debating. But their power is drastically increasing. The latchkey independents raised themselves, grew up and started businesses and families, and during the next decade they will increasingly overtake politics.

Like Shakespeare's Henry V, they partied through the teenager stage, leaving their parents appalled by generational irresponsibility and lack of ambition, and then they shocked nearly everyone with their ability and power when they suddenly decided to be adults. Now, on eve of their entrance into political power, few have any idea of the tornado ahead.

14

Beyond the Vote

Imagine what would happen if a huge chunk of citizens stopped accepting what they are told by one of the parties, stopped just aligning themselves with candidates from one of the monopoly parties, and started deeply studying, analyzing and thinking about the issues of government independently. Imagine if they shared their thoughts openly with many others, instead of just letting the news be defined by the big media responses to the big parties. Imagine the revolution that would occur in the voting citizenry.

This is exactly what happened in the decade the Internet went mainstream. It is valuable to know the profound history that led to this freedom revolution.

Keynesianism

Karl Marx agreed with Hegel that history is created by the dialectical conflict between upper classes and the masses; Lenin transferred the attention from class warfare to the conflict between rich and poor nations.[57] Most Americans and Europeans adopted this view during the Cold War. Indeed, the Cold War was the "inevitable" result of class conflict leading to conflicts between the governments of the "greedy" nations and the collectivized socialist states.

Keynes, like Lenin before him, shifted the debate by arguing that since many nations were not willing to adopt socialistic government ownership of all business the only solution was for big businesses to give people privatized "socialism" such as health insurance, savings programs (like the current 40lk in the U.S.), retirement programs and other employee benefits. Keynes further predicted that if government did things right then small businesses would be increasingly less able to offer such benefits over time and that eventually big business would run the entire economy in partnership with highly-regulating governments.[58]

Together, Keynes thought, big government and big business would phase out the disruptive, nonconformist and anti-social element of independent small business power and replace it with big corporations offering all the benefits envisioned by socialism. Simultaneously, governments would keep mavericks, entrepreneurs and innovators from rocking the boat. Socialist goals, albeit through private corporate means, would be implemented into all capitalistic nations. The result would be the end of warfare between owners and labor and the solution to most world problems.

Keynes said that once companies become so big that they are less focused on profits than appearing caring, helpful and socially responsible to the public, they will make decisions based on public relations and therefore socialistic values rather than making money. If enough big companies could be coaxed to this point, and if increased government barriers to small-business success could effectively squelch entrepreneurial initiative, even the most capitalistic nations would provide privatized "socialist" safety nets for the whole society.

In such a system, big corporations would work together with big governments to continually increase the delivery of socialistic goals such as free education for all, free health insurance for all, free health care for all, a society of employees, jobs for everyone, a meritocracy of experts ruling society, and a docile and obedient populace.

This system was adopted slowly but consistently so that Richard Nixon could announce by the mid-1970s that "we are all Keynesians now."[59] In short, Keynesianism promotes big government with high levels of regulation along with big business promoting various private offerings of socialist goals.

This social safety net has proven popular in all the Western nations, and has offered a number of short-term and positive lifestyle benefits. It has also proven a better solution than government-only socialist equivalents in one-party states like the USSR, Eastern European nations and modern Russia, China and Cuba. In multi-party nations like France and Germany some parties promote big business and others big government, and still others emphasize their pet areas of focus.

In the United States the maintenance of Keynesianism requires a major party supporting the government, a major party supporting big business, and a system of swinging back and forth between the leadership of each. When the big-government party is in power the Government-Industrial-Complex grows and when the big-business party is in power the Industrial-Government-Complex expands.

When Keynesianism is flourishing, both parties use power to increase entitlements, foreign involvements and government spending. Taxpayers and small businesses suffer.

The End of History

Francis Fukayama predicted in the 1990s that with the fall of the Berlin Wall and end of the Cold War this conflict between the rich and poor nations was over; he called this "the end of history," citing both Hegel and Marx. In the ensuing model of the 1990s, where everybody was a "capitalist," economies flourished.

With a united Germany, declining Soviet power, and the dot. com and real estate booms, everybody seemed to have forgotten

Keynesianism in the Roaring 90s. Everybody, that is, except the two big parties. Entitlements and debts grew during the Bush, Clinton, Bush and Obama Administrations. When 9/11 struck, everyone realized that history was far from over and that major challenges were still ahead. If the end of history had come, Keynes won.

Ironically, the fact that Keynesianism uses capitalistic *means* to accomplish socialistic *ends* allowed both liberals and conservatives to claim victory. Conservatives rejoiced that socialism had lost to markets, and liberals celebrated that the era of big, irresponsible capitalism was over. Unfortunately, what they brought us was far from the utopian ideal envisioned by socialism's iconic philosophers or the freedom statesmen in history. In fact, it was not so much socialism—where the state provides for all—as aristocracy, where the masses provide for the elite.

But back to our narrative: Keynesianism requires both political parties constantly and vocally doing battle. Neither can fully win nor destroy the other; and when one wins an election the other is needed to play a minority role until it can win back the majority. Whichever party is in power, the scope of government and big business must *both* increase during their tenure.

Of course, the result is that the far right hates Democrats when they are in power, and then turns on Republicans when they win and grow government. The far left does the opposite, hating the Republicans when they rule and then turning on Democrats in power for not doing enough. Mainstream members of both parties simply support their party and dislike the opposition.

The key action in all this, the thing which makes Keynesianism work, the lynchpin of the whole model, is for the citizenry to do nothing but vote. Of course, they can live their lives, work at their jobs, send their kids to school and volunteer in their community. If they do these things, plus vote, they are good citizens. No more is asked, or wanted, from them. "Just shut up and vote," is the subtle message from both parties.[60]

Of course, if one is an expert in politics, if it is their job, they are expected to do more than vote. They are required to study government, the issues and impact public opinion. The same applies to professional journalists, attorneys, professors, etc. But this only applies to professors of political science, law, public policy or a related field. Professors of literature or chemistry, for example, like postal workers and soccer coaches, are encouraged to leave governance mostly to the experts.

This cynical view is, unfortunately, widespread. Keynesianism depends on a society of experts where nearly everyone leaves governance to the political professionals. Citizens are subtly taught that voting is the role of citizenship, along with serving on a jury if called up, and to otherwise leave governance to the experts. After all, their party is watching their back for them and keeping the other "evil" party from doing too much damage. Or, if the other party becomes dangerous, their own party leadership and the media will let them know.

Responses to Being Patronized

When a few citizens realize that they are being "handled" by the professionals of their party, the first response is naturally to want to elect better party leaders. When time shows that this doesn't work, that in fact it is the nature of party leadership to spin the truth and patronize the party rank-and-file, the disillusioned party loyalist often looks to some extreme group within the party— such as the radical right or the fringe left. Alas, honest citizens find that faction leaders are usually as prone as major party heads to spin the issues and handle party members.

At this point, many party members just give up. "The other party is bad," they rationalize, "and my own party leaders are just too political. But at least candidates from my party are better than those from the other party."

Some sincere seekers actually ignore tradition and years of brainwashing and seek for a better situation in the other party. At first, party switchers may find a few things they really like better about the new party—especially if they attend in-person events and get to know some of the people in the other party. "Republicans /or/ Democrats aren't so bad," they realize.

The longer they stay with the new party, however, the more they see that both parties are run in virtually the same way, like a formula primetime program, with the same character-types inhabiting the various roles. Eventually they see most of the same problems that caused them to question their original party.

The idea that both parties are a problem is like the end of history for many voters. Most have seen politics itself as a war to put the good party in power and kick out the bad party. So when a voter realizes that both parties have serious problems, and even worse—that neither party is likely to really solve America's problems—there is a major paradigm shift.

Some give up in utter frustration, while others get really mad at their own party. Others get even angrier with the "other" party and refocus their support for their original party. But one reality remains in the minds of most people arriving at this understanding: Neither party has the answers, and neither party is likely to really fix our problems. More, the system is basically designed so that the party of big government and the party of big business take turns being in charge.

When regular citizens understand the goals of Keynesianism, it is a major shock. At this point, what is a caring, sincere and committed citizen to do? When you learn that parties are parties are parties, how do you stay involved in governance? And how do you stay positive and optimistic about the future?

The Big Decision

The answer is for citizens to begin to study and think a lot more about government and to stop ignoring freedom by leaving it to the political professionals. Unless regular people realize that freedom is up to them, not the experts, and that they need to learn more and take more action to make a real difference, they are unlikely to become true citizens. When a person does make these realizations, however, he or she drastically changes. He becomes excited about impacting freedom.

There are three major ways to do this, and the three are drastically different:

1. Populism

2. Activism

3. Independence

This is "the big decision" for free citizens who really want to maintain and even increase freedom. Whether your political views are generally liberal, conservative, libertarian, progressive, green, or centrist, the big decision is a powerful way to start making a real difference.

Here are more thoughts on the three paths of the big decision:

1. Populism. This means openly and vocally fighting the system, pointing out its flaws, and actively participating in influencing change. Populism has a long history in America, from the Populist Party movement of the 1880s and 1890s which arose because many people felt that neither of the two major parties would listen to them, to the Progressives of the early 1900s, the Labor movement of the 1920s and 1930s, or the counter-Culture revolution of the 1960s and the counter-Populism of the 1970s.[61] More recent populism includes anti-incumbency, Tea Parties, Coffee Parties, and the Green movement, among others.

2. Activism. This consists of committing to one of the major political parties and really having a powerful influence on it. While much of this book emphasizes the rise of independents, it should not be understated how valuable truly independent-thinking citizens can be if they choose to maintain strong party ties. This is not only a legitimate but also a highly needed role

of promoting freedom in our society. Both major parties need more members who really study, analyze, independently think and participate in improving party communication, leadership and impact on society.

3. Independence. This means becoming your own, personal political party—a party of one citizen. Today there are more independents in the United States than either Democrats or Republicans. Independents don't depend on any party but independently study, analyze, think, spread their influence and then vote for candidates and issues they feel will most help the nation.

Whatever your decision—whether you choose to help improve society through populism, activism or independence—note that is it vital to do certain things. Those who simply depend on party experts leave these things to others, and the result is a loss of freedom. These things include:

- making a deep study of the principles of freedom and the U.S. Constitution
- studying the history of freedom in order to truly understand current and future events within their context
- studying and analyzing current issues in depth and from many different perspectives
- considering the views of those who disagree with you and really understanding the points of merit (and not just your points of contention) in their ideas
- drawing your own independent conclusions about proposals and policies after deep study
- articulating and sharing your ideas with others
- using your influence to impact the direction of the nation on specific issues and in general

Populists are often criticized for not doing these things, but those who do can make a real, positive difference in populist circles.

Activists who commit to these things can greatly support party choices, and independents need to do these in order to have a meaningful impact.

The American founders wanted citizens to do these things, and predicted that the loss of such behaviors by the citizens would be the end of the republic. If we want our freedoms to remain and even increase, we must be the kind of citizens who deserve such freedoms.

If we leave our future to the current power of Keynesianism, we will see more of the same: on-going crises, angry and ineffective politics, increased government spending and debt, increased taxes and regulations, continuing foreign conflicts and the loss of American lives, and an inability of government to solve our major problems. The more the parties fight and the louder the conflict, the greater the power of Keynesianism. Keynesianism depends on heated arguments that drive the citizens to demand bigger government programs.

As long as the party of big business and the party of big government hold a joint monopoly on our society, voters will vote and little will change—except that debts, economic crises and problems will increase. If this is the future we want for our country, we just need to leave politics to the politicians.

In contrast, the future of freedom depends on citizens who do a lot more than just vote and serve on jury duty. It depends on citizens who do the things that bring freedom—as populists, activists or independents, but all studying and thinking independently. The American system was designed with the people as overseers of government. We all need to fulfill this role better.

We need a party of small business, a party of family, a party of entrepreneurial leadership, a party of the regular citizens, a party of freedom. The American founders had a name for such a party: Citizens. Such a party naturally occurs and grows in free society when we do our true part as citizens.

Winning Elections

In our current two-party system, independents need the two big parties. There is, of course, an Independent Party, and people have differentiated members of this party from independents by using the phrase "small 'i' independents" to denote those who aren't officially affiliated with any party.

Few independents have any interest in joining a third party. They consider this a worse option than signing up as a Democrat or Republican. Most independents share a frustration with both major parties, and they see partisanship itself as symptomatic of America's problem. Independents especially dislike the political wrangling of party battles.

But let's get one thing clear: In nearly all major elections, most independents end up voting for a candidate from one of the two big parties. There are several lessons to be learned from this.

Let's Party!

First, independents need the parties. Perhaps a non-party arrangement like the one envisioned by America's founding fathers will someday offer a better system. Or maybe independents will eventually take over one of the major parties. But in our current system independents need the parties to be and do their best. Independents need to be able to choose between the highest caliber of candidates and policies, and the sheer numbers affect both the ability to get a message out, and the ability to attract willing candidates.

Bottom line: the parties are still providing most available options for our votes.

Second, the two-party system needs independents. When the big parties hold a monopoly on political dialogue and innovation, centrist members of both parties congeal together a great deal and the parties often seem more alike than different. Throw large numbers of independents into the mix, however, and the parties are forced to energetically debate their platform and the weaknesses of their opposition's candidates, policies and so forth. They have to articulate more clearly their message and differentiate themselves in order to garner independent votes.

Ironically, as much as independents abhor political fighting, it is by contrasting themselves with such "vulgarity" that thoughtful, idealistic and principled independents define themselves. Not as a group, of course—but as individuals who are independent of and above the disingenuous and exploitive methods and motivations they believe typify the party loyalists. The noisy and unproductive debate is the point to which independents are counterpoint.

Studied, serious-minded citizens who think and act independently and make their influence felt are exactly the type of citizens the American founders hoped would populate the republic. Party loyalties too often reduce this level of independence. At their best, independents function as much-needed checks and balances on the two-party system that has become too powerful.

Party People

The independents need the parties, and the two-party *system* needs the independents. But a third lesson might be the most important. The individual parties themselves actually need independents. Political parties are only as strong as their collective members, and there are certain types of members that are extremely valuable to party influence.

For example, parties benefit from Traditionalist members—people who were raised with passionate loyalties to Democrats or Republicans. Such members nearly always vote for the party and its candidates, and often they cast straight party votes without seriously considering other options. Their allegiance to the long view of Party dominance overshadows their concerns and even outright disagreements with the Party.

Politicos are a second important group of members in any party. Politicos *love* politics. They watch it with as much interest and passion as dedicated sports fans follow their team. Politicos listen to party leaders, think about and memorize talking points and promote the party line. They also study lots of literature debunking the other party and pass along these arguments.

A third type found in both parties is the Intellectual. Intellectual Partyists are distinguished most by their habits of skepticism and asking questions. They consider party literature mere propaganda and instead search out and study original sources. Intellectuals typically read opposing party sources as much or more as works from their own party.

Policy Wonks are a fourth type in any party, and they care most about specific proposals, plans and models, and enjoy studying them in detail, discovering patterns and flaws, and creating counter-proposals and solutions. They examine, scrutinize, analyze, write, and attend lots of seminars, panels and other events filled with discussion. Most of them make their living doing these in academia, media, punditry, the lecture circuit or blogosphere, or the like.

A fifth type, Activists, are usually familiar with the other types but they put most of their effort into influencing state or federal legislative votes, agency policies, judicial cases or executive acts. They are found at all levels of government from local to international organizations. Some of them put most of their focus into elections.

Party Officios, a sixth type of party promoter, hold party positions in local precincts all the way up to national committees. Some are full-time paid professionals or experts, but the large majority of them serve voluntarily as officers, delegates, candidates, unofficial advisors and other roles in the party. Among party Officios are those holding office. These elected and appointed officials represent their party in specific positions of public service.

Seventh and eighth types are Donors and Fundraisers. They of course play important roles in all parties, since political machines are expensive, and funding often significantly influences policy and elections.

There are various other types of people that help parties succeed, but the most influential type of all is the people who could simply be called "Majorities." The obvious power of Majorities is that they have the numbers and therefore the votes to steer the party. They elect the delegates who elect the party candidates, and their influence is deeply and widely felt in general elections.

Majorities are mostly made up of regular, non-politician, thinking citizens who have the most influence on party delegates, general donations and the general voters. Majority types are usually not Traditionalists, Politicos, Officios, Wonks or political experts. But they keep track of what is happening in society and think seriously about political concerns, issues and elections. They spread their influence day after day and impact thinking widely and consistently.

The media is seldom able to predict close elections because of this wildcard: Since Majorities' type of engagement is largely internal and interpersonal, and because their influence is largely in a realm that is under-valued by (or perhaps beyond the control of) those in power, it is almost impossible to know what Majorities are really thinking and to predict how they will impact outcomes.

Winning Elections

So why do the parties need independents? At first glance, it might appear that the parties would do better if independents would just split and join the big parties. But a deeper analysis shows how significant the growth of independents has become.

Independents aren't just the new numerical majority; they are the barometer of success. As a type, independents aren't Traditionalists, Politicos or Officios. Most of them are Majorities, and a lot of them are Wonks. In short, they care little about the future of the party, and a lot about helping both people in particular, and the nation in general.

Parties need the votes of independents, but they need something more. The two big parties both need independent Majorities. When they are receiving independent support, they know that they are probably on track. Or, when they lose independents, they know to step back and reevaluate their direction.

There are certainly times when government officials need to ignore independents and everyone else and stand firm on the right path. But most times they can pretty much tell how well they are doing by finding out what the independents are thinking.

Of course, independents aren't always right. *But they are right more often than the big parties because in general, they care more about the nation than about party power!* Madison and Jefferson would applaud.

This is a great benefit to both parties. In some ways, independents have made it easy for many politicians. Win the independents, win the election.

Building and Leading the New Tribes

The Industrial Age worldview of materialistic nations and careers dominates the modern world. It has many advantages, but it also brings with it certain weaknesses and limitations. A second major worldview, Tribalism, is returning to the world, overtaking business marketing and spreading to other sectors of society. The New Tribes have few of the weaknesses of traditional tribal cultures, but still boast many of the benefits.

What great lessons from tribes do we desperately need in our modern society, and how will the New Tribes restructure business, government, the economy, families and education in the next few decades?

Perhaps most importantly, how will the emergence of New Tribes as the leading basis of society impact the future of freedom?

Why Tribes are Vital to Success in the 21ˢᵗ Century

Seth Godin's runaway bestseller _Tribes_ took a quaint anthropological label and turned it into a pop culture buzzword. And while his timely ideas helped articulate a fresh and needed approach to marketing and beyond, the power of tribal culture is far greater than any publishing or sales phenomenon. Whether he realized it or not, Godin swerved into a truth of huge ramifications—far more significant than social networks or marketing wizardry.

Tribes are not only the shape of our past, but the key to our future; and they have everything to do with freedom. Several millennia of history seem to argue that there is something both natural and functional about tribal society for human beings. And yet most moderns have little sense of its value – nor less, its relation to our freedom and our future.

Our Tribal Roots

On many occasions I have asked well-read college students, including executives and graduate students, to diagram the American government model which established unprecedented levels of freedom and prosperity to people from all backgrounds, classes and views. It's turned out to be something of a trick question, as they usually do it in the wrong order—and they invariably get the most important part wrong. Specifically, they start by diagramming three branches of government (a judicial, an executive and a bicameral legislature) and then sit down, thinking they've done the assignment.

When I ask, "What about the rest?" they are stumped for a few seconds. Then some of them have an epiphany and quickly return to the white board to diagram the same thing at the state level. This time they are sure they are done.

"What level of government came first in the American colonies?" I ask. After some debate, they agree that towns, cities and local governments were established, many with written constitutions, for over two centuries before the U.S. Constitution and many decades before the state governments and constitutions.

"So, diagram the founding model of local government," I say. They usually diagram a copy of the three-branch U.S. Constitutional model—which is entirely incorrect. This little exercise would be a whole lot more amusing if its implications were not so troubling.

This sad lack of knowledge indicates at least one thing: Americans who have learned about our constitutional model have tended to memorize it largely by rote, without truly understanding the foundational principles of freedom. We're like apes at the switch: highly trained, but with no earthly idea what all the machinery is for—or any sense of our lacking.

Civics 101

The first constitutions and governments in America were local, and there were hundreds of them. These documents were the basis of later state constitutions, and they were also the models in which early Americans learned to actively cooperate to govern themselves. Without them, the state constitutions could never have been written. Without these local and state constitutions, the U.S. Constitution would have been very, very different. In short, these local constitutions and governments were, and are, the basis of American freedoms and the whole system of Constitutional government in the United States.

The surprising thing, at least to many moderns, is that these local constitutions were very different than the state and federal constitutional model. True, they were harmonious in principle with the ideals that informed the state and federal models. And there were some similarities; but the structure was drastically different. The principles of freedom are applied distinctly at local and tribal levels to be effective.

Freedom at the Local Level

Another surprise to many is that nearly all the early townships and cities in the Americas adopted a constitutional structure very similar to *each other*. They were amazingly alike. This is because they are designed to apply the best principles of freedom to the local and tribal levels. But there is more. A similar model was followed by the Iroquois League as well, and by several other Native American tribal governments.

This same model of free local/tribal government shows up in tribes throughout Central and South America, Oceana, Africa, Asia and the historic Germanic tribes. Indeed, it is found in the Bible as followed by the Tribes of Israel; this is where the American founders said *they* found it—primarily in Deuteronomy chapter 30.

This pattern is not accidental, coincidental or imitative. It is a predictable model based on natural law and human nature; and an understanding of these leads to the establishment of efficient, effective and freedom-producing local forms. And it is these local "tribal councils" that are the roots of freedom, from which all the more complex and over-arching forms at the state and federal levels are derived. Detach these from their tribal-governance roots, and you end up with a very different outcome.

Foundations of American Freedom

The most accurate way, then, to diagram the American governmental system is to diagram the local system correctly, then the federal and state levels with their three branches each, separations of power and checks and balances. But how exactly does one diagram the local level?

The basics are as follows. The true freedom system includes establishing, as the most basic unit of society, local government councils that are small enough to include all adults in the decision-making meetings for major choices. This system is clearly described in Tocqueville's *Democracy in America*, Volume 1, Chapter 5, and in Liberty Fund's *Colonial Origins of the American Constitution*.

These town, city or tribal councils truly establish and maintain freedom by including in the most local and foundational decisions the voices and votes of all the adult citizenry. These councils make decisions by majority vote after open discussion. They also appoint mayors/chiefs, law enforcement leaders, judges and other officials. All of these officials report directly to the full council and can be removed by the voice of the council.

Representative houses and offices are much more effective at the larger state and national levels. But the point that cannot be stressed enough is: The whole system breaks down if the regular citizens aren't actively involved in governance at the most local levels.

In this model, every adult citizen is literally a government official, with the result that all citizens study the government system, their role in it, the issues and laws and cases, and think like leaders. Without this, freedom is eventually lost.

Indeed, in a nation where the government derives its just powers from the consent of the governed, is it any wonder that a population of unengaged "citizens" is the beneficiary of a government constantly increasing its power at the cost of our freedoms? What other outcome can reasonably be expected?

Once again, the most successful tribes, communities and even nations through history (like the Anglo-Saxons) have adopted this model of local governance that includes all citizens in the basic local decision-making. The result has always been increased freedom and prosperity. No free society in history has lasted once this system eroded. Tocqueville called this system of local citizen governance "the" most important piece of America's freedom model.[62]

Today we need to better understand the foundations of tribal culture so that we actually, truly begin to understand local and tribal governance in a system of freedom. I believe that this will be vital to the future of freedom in a world where the new tribes are taking the place of historical communities.

A Basic Tribal Culture

There are at least three major cultural traditions of the world's history. The three might be described in modern terms as Warriors, Farmers and Competitors.

Warrior cultures believe in enemies, battles, winners and losers, us *versus* them, strength, courage, victory, personal skill, honor, resiliency, and a bias toward action—among other things. They tend to see the world in terms of "our tribe" above all else. Many in history called themselves "the people," or "the chosen." The tribes that became the nations of Norway (Norse), England (Anglos), France (Franks), etc. were from this tradition; other examples are found around the world.

Farmer traditions valued security, hard work, frugality, sexual morality, responsibility, loyalty to community, savings and assets, land ownership, integrity, education, honesty, steadiness, family loyalty, neighborliness, and prosperity defined by abundance of food. They built communities, simultaneously promoted individual freedom and conformity to community norms, and considered themselves successful when they produced bountiful harvests and saw their children married well (to spouses who embodied the values of the community).

Competitor traditions saw the world as (usually) friendly competition between children at play, youth at courting and adults at work. Even the elderly competed to brag about the best lives, worst pain, most accomplished son, most neglectful daughter, most talented grandchildren, and whatever else came up. For example: "I have two sons who are doctors and a daughter who is a lawyer," *versus* "My grandson is a star quarterback who just won a state championship and his sister just got a scholarship from a national competition she won in Washington, D.C." People in such societies like competitive entertainment to escape from the pressures of their competitive schools and jobs.

A lot more could be said about these three major traditions, but the key point here is how they relate to tribes and freedom. Warrior societies are tribal by nature, and they grow by conquering and colonizing other societies. They see life as a big battle, and raise their children and spend their days in battle mode. They believe that life is about either conquering or being conquered. They see those with farmer and competitor traditions as victims.

Farmer societies are also tribal, but see the world as a big desert that needs to be turned into a garden. The more people who will adopt their values and join their quest to beautify and expand the garden, the better. To them, the warriors and competitors are savages and wild outsiders who should be avoided and kept away from their society.

Pitfalls of National Culture

Competitor cultures are National (as opposed to tribal): interested in education for career, working moderate hours in order to enjoy daily entertainments, uninvolved with neighbors unless there is some other relationship to pull them together, and selfish with their free time. They see the world as a big race, and individuals want to be the winners instead of the losers. In fact, they generally look down on "losers" and avoid them lest losing somehow "rub off" on them. They see warrior and farmer cultures as quaint and backward, at best, and often with a more critical eye. Clearly, those cultures aren't winning the race.

Competitor cultures divide their competitions into those that matter and those that don't. They join tribes for the ones with little at stake, but stay individually focused on the ones that matter most. Career and money are the competitions that matter more than any others in these cultures. Even family relationships have to take a back seat to most career considerations. In other words, competitor cultures *appear* tribal by habit, but are nationalistic when they feel something is really important.

National cultures therefore desperately need the lessons taught by traditional tribal cultures. But there are also pitfalls and negatives typical to tribal cultures, and we want to learn what they are and avoid them. The American founders took on a deliberate process of statecraft, weighing the merits and failings of forms, models and ideals from societies throughout history. I would assert that such a considered approach to our future as a nation and society is called for today. The goal is to adopt the best from national, tribal, warrior, farmer, competitive and other cultures, and at the same time reject their flaws and weaknesses.

The Tribal Worldview

With this in mind, let's discuss what the tribal ideal really is. With the assumption of local governance under the direction of concerned and involved citizens who were invested in one another's success and security—basically a tribal council at the community level—the American founders established constitutional forms to create a cooperative and interactive union of states.

We have lost too much of the tribal foundation that was the animating spirit of American culture—the underlying weave of the fabric of freedom—and it is hard to overstate the case for recapturing it.

Just as there are religious worldviews, secular worldviews, materialistic worldviews, etc., there is an overarching tribal worldview. Just like there are many views and differences within, say, the religious worldview, there are many different tribal perspectives. And just as there is an overarching religious worldview (there is a higher power, and I should live in harmony with it/Him), there is also a profound and powerful tribal worldview.

One of the best ways to begin to understand any worldview is to ask, "What is the world, and what is the purpose of life and the universe?" This is a complex question, of course, but it can be answered in simple terms and the early answers are often the most important. By understanding tribal culture at this basic level, we understand a great deal about ourselves.

The Universe

As I have studied tribal cultures from around the world and throughout history with these questions in mind (*What is the world? What is the purpose of life and the universe?*), I have categorized recurring themes, forces and societal roles; the labels used here are my own.

In generic tribal thought, the universe is made up of certain vital entities. For example, first come the **Obeyers**; these do their part in the universe unfailingly. They include suns, moons, planets, rocks, canyons, rivers, mountains, valleys, etc. Many ancient religious temples and writings are full of these Obeyers. Obeyers set an example to all others, and they are the basic building blocks of everything. Many ancient stories center around references to and morals learned from valleys, rivers, mountains, etc.

Next are the **Growers**: the trees, grasses, plants, fruits, and so on. They build the universe by growing. Their growth feeds the others, bringing the power of the sun into assimilable form. Many ancient religions and philosophies are built around the Growers and grower symbols.

The **Movers** include animals, fish and birds. They move around the world, spreading minerals and seeds from the Obeyers and Growers as they travel. Many tribes consider some of the movers, especially birds, to be messengers, teaching us as we interact with them in the world. They also provide food to others, and feed the Growers when they die. The Movers are a key part of the universe, as are the Growers and Obeyers.

The **Fishers** are an interesting group. They change the environment by building dams to fish like beavers, or storing nuts like squirrels. Bees and others fit this category. They somehow raise and harvest food, not just wander and search for it. In some traditions they are called farmers, and in others spiders (which weave webs to capture food). By their fishing, storing, farming, weaving, etc., they benefit the environment and all of life.

People are expected to learn from all of these parts of the universe, and to follow their good examples. Each type of entity is judged by how well it promotes and benefits life, which Obeyers, Growers, Movers and Fishers all do.

Next come the **Lovers**. Lovers benefit life to the extent that they love. When they don't love, they hurt life and all the other entities. The Lovers include all humans and also the spirits (or God, gods, and/or ancestors, depending on the tribe). Humans exist to love.

The Shadow Side

In addition to the good parts of the universe that benefit life, there are those that attack life. These include the Thieves, Murderers, Manipulators and Destroyers. **Thieves** take one's implements of life because they think it will benefit their life. They are mistaken, and cause pain for all by wrongly attacking life. **Murderers** take life in order to promote their own life, and in so doing increase total pain. Murderers are seen as worse than Thieves.

Manipulators are an interesting category, often considered to be much worse than thieves and murderers. **Manipulators** set up systems that steal or kill, but in a way that the thieves and murderers aren't directly blamed and in fact get away with it more often. Such systems include anything that skews the natural way things should be, such as class and caste systems, manipulative and deceptive laws and governments, tricky lending and business deals, etc.

In this worldview, the only thing worse than Manipulators are Destroyers. **Destroyers** are those whose very nature has changed, who no longer are fallen Lovers, but are truly motivated only by hate and pride.

Note that while Movers, Fishers and Humans can be Thieves and Murderers, only humans can become Manipulators or Destroyers. Since the very purpose of humans in the universe is to love, to bring as much love as possible into the world, it is a colossal tragedy if a Lover becomes a Manipulator or a Destroyer. By the way, in many traditions only Manipulators become Destroyers.

Now, with all this said, imagine how people in this culture feel about those who set up abusive, forced, corrupt and controlling governments, economies and laws: They are the worst of the worst. Even those who support, condone or allow such manipulative governments, laws and economies are doing the work of the Destroyers and attacking life and all that is good.

This is one reason that tribal societies so adamantly mistrust most national cultures and people: It seems to many of them that the very basis of national culture is manipulations and exploitative systems. It is also why it would be so valuable for them to learn the constitutional principles of freedom and how to apply them. But our purpose here is not to admonish the tribal cultures, but to learn from them.

Major Weaknesses of Tribalism

At this point, we should note that while traditional tribal culture does have much to teach us from its idyllic simplicity, it is far from perfect; studying its pitfalls and common flaws is also instructive. When tribes are run by small councils of all adult members, these weaknesses can be mitigated. But when tribes don't follow the leadership of councils of all adults, they turn against themselves; whatever other form of government they adopt, it becomes corrupt. When this happens, various problems arise. The problems that follow are the norm for tribes that are *not* led by councils of all adults.

Economic Control

Tribal culture generally gives a great deal of economic power to tribal leaders. Interestingly, most tribes distribute political power well between the executive (who gets power only in the face of external challenges and only for the duration of the challenge), the judicial (often a shaman and in many cultures left to families—both of which are usually independent of the executive and legislative), and run by the legislative (sometimes councils of elders, sometimes the combined adults of the tribe, sometimes both).

Of course, there are tribes that fail to follow these models, but the freest tribes use these basic systems.

Still, even with political freedoms, few historical tribes have economic freedoms. The trust of the chief, the head elder (male or female) or the shaman is often absolute. And, indeed, such leaders often adopt a sort of royal mentality where they believe that what is good for the leader's finances is good for the whole tribe. In this form, nobody sees undue control of everyone's finances and ownership as a negative. But often, it creates the loss of political freedom—including parental choices, like who should marry whom—and a strict caste system with no economic or social mobility.

Many tribes face long-term poverty for most members of the tribe. Such poverty never persists in a truly free-enterprise model, which includes both freedom *and* opportunity. Often tribal leaders see this as a threat to their power and, by extension, the tribe's security and viability.

Emerging tribes with a charismatic leader who seeks control over individuals' and families' finances are cultish, and history is littered with the tragedies that such arrangements can cause. If a tribe wants to sell things, that's great. But trying to pool resources or give up control of personal property should of course be met with serious suspicion.

This discussion also exposes a national-culture flaw: the idea that in learning from other cultures we should not judge their systems, traditions and behaviors. Perhaps this is true when the goal is to maintain purity and academic objectivity in anthropological studies, but it is certainly not true when our purpose is to learn and apply the best of tribal (and national) cultures to the tribally-nationalistic-globally-connected societies of the future.

If some calamity changes the world drastically, the same lessons will need to be applied in the new local societies that will be forged. We need to measure the parts of each culture by how well they promote and support an environment of freedom, prosperity and happiness for all.

Interpersonal Politics

In a small group, political power is often swayed by personalities, likes and dislikes, trysts and history, baggage and personal weaknesses. Nothing can keep this from happening, and in a free system and voluntary tribes it doesn't matter much. In a local or official tribal system where the government has actual power over life, death, imprisonment, finances, etc., systems should always be established that keep this from happening. By "systems" I mean written constitutions with separation of powers, checks and balances well-structured.

Class Power

Most tribes are aristocracies. This is a problem, because the class system is usually established by those in power and dominated by certain families. In a local structure, or any model where the tribe or community is non-voluntary and/or actually has government power, the solution to this is to establish a legislature of all adults in the tribe. As the tribe grows in size and geographical scope, local councils representing perhaps no more than 150 households continue to govern themselves, and may send representatives to a regional council to manage affairs of mutual interest to the coalition of local councils.

Conformity

Tribes often flounder economically and fail to grow because the people become too socially conformist. When tribes demand sameness on many levels and in nearly every aspect of life, they shut down creativity, leadership, wisdom and progress. This is natural to any group, and in national cultures it is often called "groupthink."

It is important for any group to continue learning, thinking, risking and trying. Of course, certain violent and anti-social behaviors from rape to murder and so on cannot be tolerated. But stopping criminal behavior is far different from scripting people's lives and socially enforced hyper-conformity. This also translates to a socially enforced closed-mindedness with respect to new ideas and a lack of tolerance for diversity, which lead to a stagnation of creativity and a tendency toward thought policing.

Lack of Diversity

These weaknesses of tribalism conspire to cause narrowness of thinking, along with many of the other problems listed above. On the one hand, the whole point of tribe is joining together based on commonalities. But the thing that makes tribes flourish is truly caring about each other, connecting, bonding. And connections based on both commonality (such as the shared value of freedom of choice) *and* diversity (such as the shared value of freedom of conscience) weave a much stronger fabric than one based on sameness.

Conclusion

The New Tribes of the 21st Century would do well, of course, to avoid these pitfalls. As stated, nearly all of these go away when a tribal society is governed by small councils of all adults in the tribe. If the tribe is too large for everyone to have a voice, smaller sub-councils are needed.

Historical tribes do have their weaknesses, but these also have much to teach us. Our generation of citizens needs to understand the good and the bad from the great tribes, nations and societies of history.

CHAPTER

18

Types of Tribes: Past to Future

In our day new kinds of tribes are emerging with huge potential influence, power and popularity. Indeed, the 21st Century may be the era where tribes become the most influential institutions in the world. The trends are already in play, and nearly every major institution, nation and civilization is now made up of many tribes. In fact, more people may be more loyal to their closest tribes now than to any other entity.

There are many types of tribes in the history of the world. A generic overview will obviously have its flaw and limitations— as will any inductive study, from personality typing to weather forecasting. But with the necessary disclaimers and apologies, we can still learn much from the generalizations as we seek lessons to apply to ourselves.

There are several significant types of tribes in history, including: Foraging Tribes, Nomadic Tribes, Horticultural Tribes, Agrarian Tribes (communities), Industrial Tribes, and Informational Tribes.[63] Each is very different, and it is helpful to understand both the similarities and unique features of these types of tribes.

Note that the fundamental connecting factor that kept these tribes together was their means of production and their definition of wealth. Families usually sacrificed to benefit the means of production. On a spiritual/emotional level, one way to define a tribe is a group of people who are invested in each other and help each other on an on-going basis. All these types of tribes meet this definition.

Level One Tribes: Everyone Knows Everyone

First, **Foraging Tribes** were usually established by family ties— sometimes, small family groupings and in other cases, larger groups with more extended family members. In marriage a person often left the tribe to join a new tribe. Foraging tribes lived by gathering and hunting together. Their central means of production were legs: the ability to go out and find food for the family. Children were the greatest source of wealth because they grew and provided more legs to the tribe. These tribes were often female-centric, and their gods were fertility goddesses and earth goddesses who provided bounty of food.

Nomadic Tribes hunted and gathered, but also pillaged in order to survive and prosper. They traveled, some within a set area and a few more widely ranging. They were nearly all herding societies, using animals to enhance their ability to hunt, gather and pillage. Their means of production was their speed, provided by great runners or herd animals. They usually traveled in larger groups than Foragers, and intermarried within the tribe or from spouses taken during raids. Marriage meant joining the tribe of your spouse. Nomadic Tribes were usually dominated by males and often practiced plural marriages. Herds were the central measure of wealth.

Third, **Horticultural Tribes** planted with sticks, hoes or hands, and tended crops to supplement food obtained by hunting. Because hoes and sticks can be wielded equally by men and women, these tribes were often female-centric. Men hunted and women planted and harvested, bringing an equality to production. Hands were the central means of production, used either in hunting or planting. Children were a measure of wealth, and deity was often a goddess of bounty.

These first three types of tribes make up the first level of tribal cultures, where nearly all tribe members worked each day to feed themselves and the tribe. In the second level, specialization created free time for many to work on matters that have little to do with sustenance—from education to technology to arts and craftsmanship, and even extending into higher thinking of mathematics, logic and philosophy.

Level Two Tribes: A Community You Can Count On

Agrarian Tribes began, as Ken Wilber describes it, when we stopped planting with sticks and hoes and turned to plows drawn by beasts of burden. The change is significant in at least two major ways: First, pregnant women can plant, tend and harvest with sticks and hoes, but often not with plows, cattle and horses. That is, in the latter many pregnant women were in greater danger of miscarriage. In short, in Agrarian society farming became man's work.

This changed nearly everything, since men now had a monopoly on food production and women became valued largely for reproduction. This was further influenced by the second major change to the Agrarian Age, which was that plows and animal power produced enough surplus that not everyone had to work to eat. As a result, tradesmen, artists and scholars arose as did professional tax collectors, politicians (tax-spenders), clergymen and warriors. Before the Agrarian Revolution, clergy and politicians and warriors had nearly all been the citizen-farmers-hunters themselves.

With this change came class systems, lords and ladies, kings and feudal rulers, and larger communities, city-states and nations. The store of wealth and central means of production was land, and instead of using whatever land was needed the system changed to professional surveys, deeds, licenses and other government controls.

Family traditions were also altered, as farmers found that food was scarce after lords and kings took their share. Men were allowed one wife, though the wealthy often kept as many mistresses as their status allowed. Families had fewer children in order to give more land, titles and opportunity to the eldest. Traditions of Agrarian Tribes, Communities and Nations are surprisingly similar in Europe, Asia, the Middle East and many colonies around the world.

While small Agrarian communities and locales often followed basic tribal traditions, larger cities and nations became truly *National* rather than tribal. The fundamental difference between the two is that in tribes nearly all the individuals work together frequently on the same goals and build tight bonds of love and care for each other, while in nations there is much shared history and common goals but few people know each other or work together regularly.

As society nationalized, most people still lived and loved in tribal-sized communities. Whether the ethnic communities of European cities, the farming villages of the frontier, church units of a few hundred who worshipped but also bonded together throughout the week, or so many other examples, most people during the Agrarian Age were loyal to national government but much more closely bonded with members of a local community.

When life brought difficulties or challenges, it was these community tribal members that could be counted on to help, comfort, commiserate, or just roll up their sleeves and go to work fixing their neighbors' problems.

Community was also where people turned for fun and entertainment. For example, one great study compared the way people in mid-century Chicago watched baseball games, attended cookouts and nearly always went bowling in groups, to the 1990s where most Americans were more likely to watch a game on TV, grill alone and go bowling alone or with a non-family friend.

Level Three Tribes: Cooperating for a Paycheck

Indeed, by the 1990s America was deeply into the Industrial Age. **Industrial tribes** (no longer really Tribes, but rather tribes, small "t") were built around career. People left the farms, and the communities that connected them, for economic opportunities in the cities and suburbs. Some ethnicities, churches and even gangs maintained community-type tribes, but most people joined a different kind of tribe: in the workplace.

The means of production and measure of wealth in Industrial tribes was capital. The more capital you could get invested, the better your tribe fared (at least for a while) *versus* other tribes. Competition was the name of the game. Higher capital investment meant better paychecks and perks, more job security, and a brighter future—or so the theory went. While it lasted, this system was good for those who turned professional education into a lucrative career.

With level three came new rules of tribe membership. For example, individuals in industrial societies were able and even encouraged to join multiple tribes. Where this had been possible in Agrarian communities, nearly everyone still enjoyed a central or main community connection. But in the Industrial era, everyone joined long lists of tribes. In addition to your work colleagues, Industrial professionals also had alma-maters, lunch clubs like the Kiwanis or Rotarians, professional associations like the AMA or ABA or one of the many others, and so on.

With your kids in soccer, you became part of a tribe with other team parents; same with the boy scouts and girls clubs. Your tribes probably included a community fundraiser club, donors to the post office Christmas food drive, PTA or home school co-op (or both), church committees, car pool group, racquetball partners, biking team, local theatre, the kids' choir, lunch with your friends, Cubs or Yankees fans, and the list goes on and on and on. In level three, the more tribes the better!

The two major tribes that nearly everybody joined in Industrial society were work tribes and tribes of friends. Between these two, little time was left for much besides work and entertainment. But make no mistake, the guiding force in such a society—the central tribe that all the others were required to give way for—was making the paycheck. Families moved, children's lives conformed, marriages sacrificed, and friends changed if one's work demanded it. It was not always so, and this morality defined Industrial Age culture.

One big downside to Paycheck Tribes is that they cared about your work but not so much about *you*. Indeed, this is one of the main reasons why Industrial tribes weren't really even tribes. The other major reason is that most people had only a few close friends and didn't truly count on any non-family group or neighborhood or community to really be there for them when they needed it. That's why this is called National society—because it's not a tribal community of bonded, connected people who truly love you and will take a stand for you.

Of course, there are some who build and maintain fabulous agrarian-type relationships, friendships and communities during Industrial eras. It is just harder and less naturally occurring than in the other types of tribal periods and places. The main reason for this may be simply that capital is less naturally connective than legs, hands, family, church or a caring neighborhood.

This is not to say that companies can't care, love and connect. In fact, I think that is exactly what they'll have to do to truly succeed in the Information Age. However, connecting, caring and building relationships is less valued during Industrial Ages. Those who put family, friends and other vital relationships first find much happiness and community connection during any period of history.

Fortunately, we live in a time when the new *e*-tribes are growing and increasingly available.

New Tribes: A Fourth Level

The sixth type of tribe is the Information-Age Tribe. We are all still struggling for the perfect name. The term "*e*-tribe" is too narrow, since many of the new relationships are not online. I think I'll settle for calling them the New Tribes, and let the future show us exactly how they turn out.

The New Tribes appear to be a whole new (fourth) level of tribe, for a number of reasons. To begin with, people are joining many of them like during Industrial times, but also limiting them somewhat to reflect what is truly important to them.

For example, where in levels 1-2 people belonged almost exclusively to one tribe and in level 3 they joined dozens of tribes, now most New Tribers are active members of a few, important tribes, often four or more per person.

In addition, many members of New Tribes want to be leaders in tribes, and many leaders of New Tribes want the members to all lead. That's a huge improvement on levels 1-3.

Also, members of New Tribes seem to care about each other much more than Industrial tribes but also even more than many ancient-style and agrarian tribes. I think this is because people had little say about whom their tribal and community members and neighbors were down through history, but in the New Tribes you can make your very best friends your daily confidantes. The interaction is powerful, and it can and does create deep bonds of friendship and caring.

The Future of New Tribes

Few people realize how widespread the New Tribe revolution has become. The many examples of online New Tribes show how rapidly this trend is growing. But there is even more to it than that. One cycle of business growth says that all new things go through four levels: first they are ignored, then they are laughed at, then they are opposed, and finally they are accepted as obvious. The growth of New Tribes is at the Obvious stage.

For example, tribal currency is now the most widely used money in the world. That may surprise some people who believe that the dollar or the yen or some other national currency is most used. But try this experiment. Pull out your wallet or planner, and see how much money you have in government-printed currency.

Then see how much you have available in private bank currency (checks or debit cards). Finally, how much are you carrying in tribal currency (from, say, the Visa or MasterCard tribes, or Discover or American Express)? While it is true that these private currencies exchange into government money, the truth is that your credit account is most likely a niche or tribal account rather than a government account.

And I dare say that more than a few readers are befuddled by this example, as they transact very few purchases by pulling out their wallet, with the actual plastic in hand; they most often buy over the phone or online—further making the point.

The significance of this is huge. How much wealth are you carrying in sky miles, for example? Or hotel or travel points? The reason companies issue loyalty cards is to get you to stop being in the traveler niche and instead join the Delta or British Airways tribe. While you still have your wallet or purse out, look through it to see how many tribal membership and customer loyalty cards you carry. Costco? Sam's Club? An automobile club? What else? Do you carry a church card, or a school card? What about other online commerce tribes like Amazon Prime, Staples Rewards, etc.?

The point of all this is that New Tribes are here to stay, and indeed that before the 21st Century ends they may well take over many roles that were traditionally governmental. For example, the phrase "I'll fedex it" has replaced "I'll mail it" in many corporate circles (to be later supplanted by "YouSendIt" and "Google Docs"), and toll roads are becoming more popular around the world. Just like government railways were phased out by private airlines, look for the rise of many more tribally-led industries and services in the years and decades ahead.

For New Tribes to fully achieve their positive potential, it is helpful and perhaps essential for them to learn from the best lessons of the tribes throughout history. Both leaders and participants of tribes gain much wisdom by studying the best practices and traditions of the world's tribes. This is the focus of the next chapter.

Tribal vs. National

National and tribal societies have much to learn from each other. Unfortunately, national cultures tend to ignore tribal lessons due to a sense of superiority and the feeling that "primitive" cultures can't have much to teach us. This arrogance has cost us much over the centuries. Indeed, our biggest challenges today are nearly all strengths in traditionally tribal cultures.

In a similar fashion, many in tribal cultures refuse to learn from national societies because they consider them exploitive, untrustworthy, alien, manipulative, spiritually unenlightened and even unworthy or inferior. Over the years, I have worked with a number of friends from tribal backgrounds who have shared their great goal of "helping their people." Sadly, their wisdom is often rejected because so many of their people refuse to accept ideas even remotely influenced by national viewpoints or people.

There are many examples of great visionaries and leaders from both national and tribal cultures that have risen above these challenges. We need more leaders from both groups to do the same. In candor, though, I admit that my purpose in researching and writing this is to help national cultures learn the vital lessons taught by tribes.

I am also convinced by the trends and evidence that a new type of tribe is arising and will soon rival governments, states and even families for influence in society. In fact, in the lives of literally millions of Internet users, this is already occurring.

We are living through a shift in focus as significant as America's move from British colony to independent nation or from westward pioneering to industrialism and nationalism. This shift will impact nearly every aspect of our lives, bringing with it new institutions and new issues far into our future.

America's Societal Evolution

America's focus on nationalism that began under Theodore Roosevelt was replaced during World War II with widespread internationalism, and after the War the United States spent over three decades building and strengthening international institutions and relationships.

During the Cold War, conservatives and liberals heatedly debated the goals of government in the United States; but most agreed on its growing role around the world. Indeed, only the extreme right and far left promoted nationalism, which was usually called "isolationism," "extremism" or "radicalism" by mainstream Republicans and Democrats.

With the fall of the Berlin Wall in 1989, internationalism was quickly succeeded by globalism. The difference between the two is that internationalists still recognize individual nations as the key actors in the global community, while globalists promote the increasing power of extra-national organizations over nations. For the so-called "isolationists," internationalism and globalism are often seen as the same thing, but the differences are significant.

Businesses followed this same pattern, emphasizing local and state growth in the 19th Century, going national in the 1920s and beyond, and then taking their goods and services international after 1945. During the Internet era, corporations went truly global, sometimes rivaling governments in resources and power and increasingly influencing world events.

A New Type of Community

Today a new ideal is gaining momentum, both politically and economically. It is oriented toward global markets and growth, and also to local community connections and even the creation of online communities that connect, care, interact almost daily, and bond.

For a long time, conservatives have touted the value of such local communities; and liberals have argued that "it takes a village" to meet our basic individual and family needs. But the new communities that are emerging are beyond what either side envisioned.

Increasingly, such local and virtual communities and networks are seeking to do more that historically has been done by one's employer, government or neighborhood friends. Indeed, many people today, perhaps most people in developed nations, have more real friends online than in the ten-mile or even hundred-kilometer area surrounding their home. This is certainly the case in the United States.

This is a truly new development in history. A number of thinkers have named this new model "Glocalism," the combination of local connection and global inclusion. In many ethnic tribes, small and strongly connected religious units, and developing nations, this concept of glocalism is quite accurate. But it fails to fully or clearly describe the internet/cell-phone/technological e-communities that are rapidly growing.

Tribes have traditionally been geographically centralized, dominated by strong leaders and often immobile class systems, frequently intolerant and non-inclusive, and usually lacking in economic upward-mobility. None of these characterize the new tribes. Where ancient tribes grew from families, the new tribes are mostly developing among market and interest niches.

Niches

People join niches by showing interest in something in common with somebody else. For example, attending a seminar sponsored by an organization will likely land you on their mailing list. Everyone on their mailing list belongs to their niche. But with a niche, your only interaction may be receiving a newsletter or sales material from the institution. You receive it along with others of the niche, and you may or may not get more involved. As long as your relationship with the niche goes through a central organization, you are part of a niche. Most people belong to many niches, some known and others not known.

As soon as you deeply connect with other members of the niche, or bring close friends or loved-ones to the niche, you start to think more tribally. When your relationship(s) with one person or more in a given niche reach the point that you deeply care about these people, and they about you, you are part of a new tribe.

You may or may not share several niches with people in your tribe, but deep connection, bonding, and significant personal investment in a common life goal, interest or activity are the foundational characteristics of tribe.

Tribal Power

To date, the new tribes are a voluntary social connection, and as such they have brought relatively little attention to themselves or to their potential future power—except to marketers. This will likely change as they continue to grow.

The great challenge of the American Founders was to figure out how to establish the principles of freedom in a society with both state-level and federal-level governments, while keeping both strong. The freedom challenge of our century will include implementing freedom principles in a society with governments and markets operating (at times independently, at times interactively) at the local, state, national, global *and* virtual level—*all simultaneously*.

For nearly a century now, the leading minds and programs have tended to emphasize bigger and bigger institutions; but this century may well be a period of local and tribal leadership. Even if major changes result in the shutting down or weakening of virtual communities, the locale will likely dominate.

It is past time that we should understand how to implement freedom both tribally and nationally. People who don't understand freedom lose it. More to the point, power will continue to centralize unless people at local levels know how to implement positive governance and leadership. Two hundred years ago the American founders taught a locally-oriented tribal-type populace how to apply freedom principles nationally. Today we have not only lost much of what they tried to accomplish at a national level, but most people today don't know how to apply the principles of freedom on a local/tribal level.

Lessons of Tribes

The first great lesson from tribes is of course the system of local governance being firmly based on small councils run by all adult citizens in the society. The importance of this model cannot be overstated! Without this system actively operating, freedom cannot be maintained. A second great lesson from tribal culture is the concept of *sharing* as the basis of economics.

If you come from a national background, try putting aside your skepticism for a minute and simply consider this idea. The universe gives us so many things for free: the sun, water, life, and the very air we breathe. Stop reading for a few seconds and take a long, deep breath.

Now take another.

How does that feel? The universe just shared it with you, free of charge. Next time it rains, try standing outside for a few minutes with your face raised to the sky and just letting the raindrops fall on your face. Again, they are shared with you freely.

Of course, this is where one's nationalistic background kicks in with thoughts like: "Fine, I like a deep breath or raindrops on my face, but that's hardly the basis of an economic system," or "How can anyone really believe that we can build a whole system on the idea of sharing? That's way too idealistic."

Both of these thoughts and others like them betray an interesting weakness of national culture: It has the propensity to try to systemize everything, to believe that only things that can be structured and repeated are valuable. But tribal culture teaches something very different: That one deep breath is of value just for its own sake, even if you only do it that one time and never set up any system or habit of deep breathing.

Likewise, that one experience with the rain falling on your upturned face is a great experience, regardless of whether or not you ever repeat it or schedule "stand in rain" periods in your electronic planner.

That's what sharing is all about. Arguably, a complex economy cannot be built on sharing; the fact that special constructs and ordered systems are needed beyond simple sharing is interpreted by national culture as an argument against it; but tribal culture doesn't even wonder if sharing with a friend or even a stranger will change the world. Tribal culture shares because a person needs something, and you can help. Period. Why does there need to be a system or model or rule for this? Why not just share when the opportunity arises?

The fact is that the result of such abundant thinking would greatly improve the economy (not to mention the metaphysical benefits to tribal bonds, and the practical benefits to those on the receiving end); and modern-day abundance gurus (contenders for the role of our shaman?) would also predict that it will actually be more effective if those choosing to share aren't deliberately mindful of the boost to the system, but rather just spontaneously helping when they see a need.

A third lesson, also in the realm of economics, is that the greatest material value in our lives is the earth. Since this has been highly politicized in the current national dialog, it can be challenging to see past the politics and really consider the core idea. In truth, the earth is our greatest physical resource. Without the water, sun and air nothing else would matter at all for very long.

This says nothing about government policy, environmental proposals, or anything political. It is the simple truth that the earth has great, great value. Tribal culture is much less concerned with governmental initiatives concerning the environment and much more about the moral and spiritual implications of how we individually treat the earth.

I learned the fourth lesson during a weeklong seminar with a great shaman.[64] After a week of fabulous experiences and training on tribal and shamanic culture, the shaman asked us to share the most important things we had learned during the week. When it was my turn, I shared how touched I had been during the week (throughout which individual participants took turns offering the gathering prayers, according to their various religious traditions—from Jewish, to Christian, to unlabeled-seeker-of-truth) that nearly every prayer offered by the shaman thanked the earth for having enough food to eat today, warm clothes to wear, and shelter from the elements.

These small and simple things are actually profound. National cultures are often so focused on self-reliance we forget to give thanks for Providence. We have so much, and too often we take it for granted. Yet a thankful society naturally obtains a prosperous economy: it is less wasteful, more resourceful, more teachable and more resilient. It is a historical law of economics that when we are thankful we prosper, while those who are unthankful often lose much of what they have.

I do not share this shaman's religion, but I certainly share his feelings of gratitude for the little things in life. I am so thankful to him for reinforcing for me this principle by his example. National societies need to be reminded to make a habit of daily and even hourly mindfulness and gratitude.

A fifth lesson is to engage risk. Tribal culture actually rewards this attribute in its youth, whereas most national cultures (lip-service to the contrary notwithstanding) teach their young to avoid risk, failure and the lessons learned by aiming high and sometimes falling short. Ironically, the places national cultures do emphasize risk in education are tribally-oriented activities like sports, theater or debate. In academics and career, we tend to minimize risk and avoid learning the lessons of failure.

Even when young people do fail, many parents step in and try to shelter their children from experiencing the consequences and thereby learning the lessons of their choices.

This lesson is illustrated by the tribal attitude toward darkness. In tribes, people grow up sitting long outside at night in the darkness, watching the stars and embracing the shadows around them. For tribal cultures, darkness is natural, failure is a great teacher, and risk is exhilarating. In national cultures, by contrast, we value turning on the lights and coming inside when it gets dark. We even surround our back yards and patios with flood-lights so we can dispel any darkness.

If it seems that I'm overstating this point, consider the truly risk-focused career in national society: Entrepreneurship. Few parents or grandparents highly recommend this course to their children. The national view of Entrepreneurship is that it is too hard and too risky. Those who succeed at it are seen by most as mavericks, specially gifted—even geniuses. The general view is that few regular people can become successful entrepreneurs and that most should not even try. Those who feel the call to break out on their own and follow the normal and natural process of learning through failures are often looked down upon by spous-es, parents, in-laws and neighbors.

Graduating classes are often told that they can do anything, that the sky is the limit, but in one-on-one meetings nearly everyone is counseled to do things the "normal" way and to avoid risk. "Aim high, but stay safe" seems to be the national mantra. In contrast, the old-style tribal motto of "conform, conform, conform" has evolved into a New Tribal culture of "Find your true greatness and do whatever it takes to achieve your life mission!"

There is a great South Pacific tribal story of a man who wonders what to do with his life. His answer as he goes on his vision quest is, "Put your hand in the hand of God, turn your back to the fire, and then walk boldly out of the light and into the darkness." The first time I heard this story, it helped me make an important decision in my life. It has helped many others through the centuries.

A sixth lesson is to follow the call of your life's dreams. One powerful feature of traditional tribal cultures is that so many of them have non-political and non-bureaucratic religions. Most tribes have one shaman at a time, and a new shaman is chosen by the old shaman years before the old shaman passes on. Thus there is little politics involved, and literally no bureaucracy.

In this system, one of the central roles of the shaman is to help each tribe member identify his or her life mission and prepare for it. Rites of passage into adulthood often include identifying a personal totem or life guide, or even going through an ordeal or vision quest to define the individual's path and purpose.

A seventh lesson from Tribal cultures is that we should all plant seeds, nurture and help them grow to harvest, and then use their bounty to help others. Where originally this literally referred to planting, it applies today in all of our important endeavors in life. We need to trust the law of the harvest, expect to sow what we reap, and keep nurturing a project until our work is complete and it is time to move on.

Also, we need to remember always that the purpose of our life missions is not just self-gratification but more importantly truly serving and helping others. If our missions ever become all about us, then we need to re-evaluate and refocus on what is really important.

One of the major differences between tribal and national cultures is that the first tends toward public virtue, or valuing and sacrificing personal benefit for the good of the community, while the latter emphasizes putting yourself first. Of course, either of these can be taken to negative extremes, but the ideal of tribal culture is to appropriately give your life to serve and help others.

An eighth lesson is balance—that as you achieve your life mission, it is so important along the way to help others achieve their missions. Too much focus on your own mission causes you to miss out on much of life, especially important relationships.

Imagine the impact on the economy of applying these lessons:

1. Participate in Local Government Council

2. Share

3. Value the Earth

4. Give Thanks

5. Take Risks and Learn from Failures

6. Find Your True Purpose

7. Embrace the Law of the Harvest

8. Help Others Achieve Their Mission

While the tribal goal is not to establish a system or duplicable model like nationalists naturally seek, the simple application of these personal lessons in your life and by many in a society will have powerful, positive economic impact.

Lessons on Happiness

Perhaps the most important lessons on governance and economics are the lessons on happiness. Happy people are, well, *happy*. This is the ultimate goal. We aren't happy in order to be free and prosperous, but rather we value freedom and prosperity because it allows us to enjoy our happiness.

Unfortunately, many people in national cultures have tended to put more emphasis on "pursuit" than on happiness. Tribal culture has so much to teach us about happiness. From the Tibetan arts[65] to Eastern gurus[66] to the various Tribal and shamanic traditions and suggestions for happiness, Tribal cultures can teach us a great deal on how to be happy; and curiously, these values and ideals are harmonious with, and many would say they were actually originated and then lost from, the traditions and teachings on which our Western religious practices and creeds are based.

In national cultures, we often spend our time seeking the *precursors* to happiness. We think that when we are older we'll be happy; when we're wealthier we'll be happy; or when we get thinner, stronger, healthier, then we'll be happy, etc. Pretty much we seriously plan to be happy *later.*

A ninth lesson from Tribal culture is that to find happiness, we should *be happy.* If this sounds like an Asian proverb, it's because it is.[67] Tribal proverbs contain some of the best lessons. If we want to be happy, instead of trying to find that magic something that will make us happy, we should make happiness not only our purpose, but also our way of life. But how? The answers differ by tribe, including religions as tribes, but there are a number of things that most tribal cultures agree on. Lessons 10-12 contain a few of them.

A Tenth lesson is that spirituality is the basis of life. This seems obvious, perhaps, to religious people, but it is also a powerful lesson for atheists and secularists. The way you feel in your heart, your core, is so important. Forgiveness, Gratitude, Humility, Integrity, Service, Sacrifice—the virtues commonly taught as the domain of a religious life—are the key to our happiness, peace, joy, and contentment. As Virgil (who grew up in Tribal society and watched his country turn to nationalism) taught, we can never find happiness if we turn against our own soul and who we really are.[68]

Later, the Emperor Aurelius, who watched as national Rome started breaking up into smaller tribes, taught that things of passing pleasure often bring lasting pain, while things that require discipline, morality and work now nearly always translate into lasting happiness in life.[69]

An Eleventh lesson is that family should be the center of life. This has direct impact on one's happiness. Of course, it is not just family relationships but how much we invest ourselves (and the quality of that investment) in them that determine the level of our happiness. One of the topics where tribal cultures have the most to teach national societies is in family relationships and roles. Family is certainly a vital part of increasing happiness.

A Twelfth lesson of tribes is that personal mission is the central purpose of life. While most moderns don't go off into the wilderness on a vision quest to find their life purpose, perhaps more of us should do the equivalent. Without mission, life is confusing and ultimately disappointing. With a clear sense of purpose, everything in life improves.

Here are a few other great lessons those of us in nationalized culture can learn from tribal society:

- Slow down and enjoy life more, by taking siesta, enjoying long evening suppers with family and friends, and following other relaxing traditions.

- Use laughter as the first and most reliable medicine for any illness.

- Spend more time relaxing in nature.

- Change your daily routines with the seasons.

- Connect with today. For example, many tribal cultures believe that a rainy day has a different purpose for us than a sunny one.

- Experience the outdoors daily—whatever the weather may bring.

- Connect with the light and the darkness. Sleep from dusk to dawn.

- Walk outside daily, receiving nourishment from the sun and fortifying the body with natural movement such as exploring natural wonders or cultivating the earth.
- Trust in the abundance of life, seeing whatever happens as full of purpose.
- Quiet the over-active mind, and do less analyzing, worrying and judging.
- Open the heart to God, or the universe if you prefer, and really listen.
- Adopt humility in order to increase your freedom and happiness.
- Visualize your best future and believe it.
- Embrace hope, accept healing, and laugh a lot.
- Feel connected to the trees, flowers, animals, mountains, lakes, rivers, birds, sunrises, sunsets, the four directions, oceans, and so on.
- Find opportunities to change your point of view: look far into the distance, look down upon a valley, up through a canyon, around from a treetop, etc.
- Spend a lot of time in silence and solitude.
- Connect your body, heart and soul.
- Seek happiness and feelings of harmony at all times.
- Spend time finding your true purpose in life and maintain clarity of purpose.
- Take in the colors and sounds of the wind.
- Breathe deeply outside after it rains.
- Ask for what you need.
- Feel gratitude and give thanks constantly.
- Dance with joy in the evenings.
- Feel at home in your body, wherever you are.

- Share long dialogues with friends: for fun, for learning, for inspiration, for self-knowing, for supportive listening, etc.

And, of course, there are many, many more. If these seem too abstract or too foreign, remember that the great challenges of modern life are to relax, be at peace, truly and deeply connect with all the right people and things, and really feel happy and content. These are powerful lessons needed in national cultures.

A Return to Tribal Education

In the history of the world, children were traditionally raised by the whole family, not just their parents. We can learn a lot by studying tribal education and family culture. While each tribe is unique, there are a number of similarities. While these are generalities, they are often deep and profound. For example, consider the following tribal/community roles in raising a child:

Grandparents. As the elders of the tribe, Grandparents kept the history (often in oral traditions and epics) and taught it to the generations that followed. Their primary role was teaching. Indeed, they taught the children everything that is most important. They taught the basics, with hands-on training and also the sharing of stories and family culture. They taught lessons of right and wrong, good and bad, and how to tell the difference between true and false. They taught youth to work, to love, to serve, to sacrifice. They taught by example and also by precept.

Fathers. Father's role included loving and serving his wife and nurturing, providing for and protecting their children. A key part of this protection was emotional—to help form a healthy self-image in the children and instill confidence, courage, honesty and a willing heart in them. With other members of the tribe acting as teachers and disciplinarians, fathers emphasized positives. In many tribes, Fathers (and indeed all adults and children) answered to the grandparents for how they acted in their role.

Mothers. Mother's role included loving and serving her husband and nurturing, providing for and protecting their children. Mothers schooled the heart in the habits of trust and abundance, forgiveness, patience, self-discipline and service, among others. Mothers safeguarded the healthy transitions of the child from infant to small child, to pre-adolescent, and so on, until the child was an independent adult. Mothers were the daily embodiment of public virtue and the whisper of truth to their children. They instilled in them the vision that each had a sacred purpose and the conviction that each was uniquely gifted to accomplish their mission.

Uncles. For boys of many tribes, Uncles were vital mentors. They taught skills and knowledge, and passed on the culture of manhood (whether the tradition was as a warrior, a farmer or a tradesman). Boys were often more open to learning lessons from uncles because the approval of their fathers was not on the line as they learned through failure, trial and error, and repetition. For girls of the tribe, Uncles represented the model for the masculine ideal as they anticipated their roles of wife and mother. By safeguarding their hearts in a non-parental relationship that was healthy and unconditionally loving, girls learned to aspire to feminine ideals of goodness, usefulness and love freely shared with everyone. Uncles helped prepare youth for adulthood.

Aunts. They served the same mentoring role for girls as uncles did for boys. They taught the skills of food cultivation, preparation, and preservation, the making of clothing, tools, household implements, bedding and homes. They often worked in groups to prepare food for the tribe as a whole. They took turns serving and being served by the other women in the tribe as the demands of pregnancy, labor and delivery, and childcare shifted work from the needy to the able, in cycles. Beyond this, aunts in many tribal cultures were the moral compass and primary disciplinarians.

They taught children the rules, and often gave instruction, correction and consequences to misbehavior more fairly, consistently and less emotionally than parents.

Older Siblings. Their role was to be an example. By doing this, they acted as another parent and also practiced being adults. With their nascent skills and knowledge and their synchronicity with the rhythms and work of the tribe, they set the tone and showed the way for younger children to follow.

Younger Siblings. Their role was to provide practice for older siblings. They provided friendship, entertainment, play and workmates.

Cousins. Their roles were friendship, play, entertainment, work, example, protection and teaching.

Tribal Adults. Their role with the tribe's children was to set an example, teach, love and protect. Their role with the other adults in the tribe was friendship, play, work, bonding, support, help.

Clans/Totems. These were like modern service clubs. Their role was to help mentor, teach, train and educate adults in an ongoing fashion.

Tribal Shamans. Shamans were the original doctors (healers) and minstrels (poets, singers, performers). In the national world, these are often seen as two ends of the spectrum, the hard sciences *versus* fantasy on screen. Both are powerful: the scientist and the artist. They are even more powerful when combined.

Shamans often dressed up, added makeup, and acted out stories in a way that swayed and changed the minds of the tribe. By framing the way tribal members saw happenings in the world, they held huge influence.

Shamans also diagnosed illness, sought causes and prescribed treatments. As they did this, they often required patients to wait for treatment (in order to prove sincerity), held a monopoly on who could be a new shaman (the original licensing), and dispensed herbal and other chemical compounds as treatments.

They were also psychological and life counselors, sending the young on vision quests and then helping them interpret the meaning of such quests, and providing meaning to people's experiences and challenges.

Shamans were the religious leaders, like rabbis or ministers. Their central skill was fighting negative energy, whether that was fear or mistrust in the tribe, the dark energy of sickness, or the spiritual supporters of their enemies in war.

Consider, for example, the story of Elijah in the Bible, telling his young apprentice, "those [spiritual forces] with us are more than those with him."[70] Why was Elijah on the hill watching the battle when a war was at hand, why did he have a young apprentice with him, and why were they watching the spiritual forces? All of this is traditional shamanic culture. Those who know what to look for in tribal culture find it in many classics and historical events.

Chiefs. Their role was to lead the tribe in times of crisis and keep the young and the whole tribe safe.

It Takes a Parent

By understanding this division of labor and the many roles and objectives collectively served by the members of a tribe, we gain clarity—and a virtual to-do list—in our effort to effectively rear our families. In our modern world, most parents are trying to fulfill all of these roles *themselves*. They believe their job is to teach, discipline, nurture, provide, protect, instill vision, instill confidence, mentor skills, set the example, be a playmate and workmate, be a friend, teach the most important things and also life skills, heal, lead, counsel, entertain, shelter from crisis, keep away enemies, maintain safety and more.

In short, as parents we have attempted the impossible. No wonder we feel overwhelmed. It would be great if we could get tribal support to do all this, but seldom do the public schools, social services or even tightly-knit church communities take up enough of the slack. So parents do the best they can, often wondering if they'll ever measure up, and pass on to their children a legacy of anxiety, futility and "I'm-never-good-enough". This sorry inheritance is a self-perpetuating insufficiency, and the two common responses (try harder or don't even try at all) will never fully accomplish the goods or fulfill the needs in the way that we seem to be hard-wired to expect.

What is the answer for such parents, especially in a world beyond tribal supports? Some parents have just delegated it all, hoping that the public schools and services will raise their children. But this seldom works, and sometimes makes things worse as the public sector sees the need to raise the parents as well as the kids.

Building Your Community

To a large extent we *can* adopt some tribal ideals and models in our homes and communities.[71] For example, maybe dad will teach, nurture, provide, protect and instill confidence while mom agrees to teach, nurture, provide, protect and instill vision. In a carefully considered environment, older siblings can be raised to value their role in a tribal tradition.

Many couples find that they accomplish some of these challenging roles best as a team: discipline as a team, heal as a team, plan and deliver entertainment as a team, etc. Of course, as a team, parents can utilize experts for health care, special training such as music or sports, and so on.

Parents also usually find that they do best when they get involved with their extended family, a community or an *e*-tribe (or combinations of these) that help fill all the needed roles to successfully raise their kids. Community, church, *e*-tribe and others sponsor classes, events, youth conferences and other services. These are more available now than ever before in history. *E*-tribes are more easily utilized than historical tribes, and there are now thousands of options available to every family and student.

In the growing return to tribal education, parents and youth are personalizing their educational approach to meet their individual needs in schooling and other facets of life. They are searching out options online and in their local areas, and picking and choosing those things they consider to be the best fit for each child.

Filling Your Community with the Tribes You Need

For example, friends of mine left a big city to raise their family in a small town. They had home schooled their children in the urban setting, but were informed by their new rural neighbors that the local schools were very good. The parents arranged a meeting with the local public school principal and went with a list of questions.

"How is your Latin program?" "What about Mandarin?" "What is the average SAT score of your seniors, and what is the high score you've ever had?" "How many of your students have been published?" The list was long.

At the beginning of the meeting, the Principal's attitude could be summed up as a bit arrogant: "Public schools are the best, and home school is inferior and reactionary." By the time the meeting was completed, the Principal was amiably recommending that the family use online Latin courses, a distance course in calculus from a university, and writing classes online.

The parents did these things, along with enrolling some of their youth in sports, theater, and debate classes at the high school. They also engaged a local who spoke Mandarin to mentor one youth.

In truth, I think these parents went to the meeting at the school with their own smug belief in the superiority of home school. But as they talked with the principal, they learned that he had some excellent things to offer. Fortunately for the students, both the parents and the principal opened themselves, listened and really learned.

In short, this family identified each child's needs, researched the available options, and filled their community with the niches and tribes they felt most likely to meet their needs. This is the new power of tribes in education, a return to tribes with all the best features but few of the worst.

This is a growing trend. As a report in Harper's put it:

"It might at first seem that the experience of youth is now sharply divided between the old world of school and parents and the new world of social networking on the Internet, but actually school now belongs on the new side of the ledger."[72]

The new world of e-tribes for youth is now social networking and learning online, with old-line schooling considered a relic from the past for many of the rising generation.

As more and more options are available, people are joining multiple tribes to help their families and themselves succeed in their educational, career, entertainment and other endeavors.

But what about that deep sense of connection, caring, loving friends who will help you when you need it most? What about true tribal bonding, true community? Can these be created in New Tribes?

The Deeply Caring Community of New Tribes

The resounding answer is yes. I know this not only from the many examples I have read, but also from personal experience. Service to New Tribe friends may seem more difficult when they don't live next door or around the block, but in fact the power of the Internet can greatly help.

For example, when one of my children was injured in a car accident and struggling for his life at the hospital, I received literally thousands of emails and notes from people all over the world. This was started by my New Tribe friends, who passed messages and requests for prayers to their many niche and tribal connections until the whole thing snowballed. To this day I am amazed at the number and divergence of type of those who comment on how long and fervently they/their children/their meditation group/their church group prayed for my son and our family.

I was the driver of the car, and I have deep and tender feelings about this terrible incident. I also have equally deep and profound memories about the great outpouring of love our family received. I have no idea how many prayers and days of fasting were dedicated to my son and our family, but I know the number is huge. Some of my New Tribe friends who are secularists sent flowers and notes, and many people blessed and helped us in so many ways. I will never forget the outpouring of love I experienced from people I learned I could truly count on in times of need.

My wife recalls that while she was attending to our son night and day at the hospital four hours from our home, she was often asked by doctors, nurses, social workers and others how the family at home was managing, how our other five very young children could stand to have her away for over a month, etc. They were astonished at her peace and confidence that they were in good hands as literally dozens of families in our local "tribe" (consisting of our family, church and community of friends) helped with our children, finances and ministered to our emotional pain. To this day, some our children's fondest memories are of the ministrations by the "Aunts," "Uncles," "Cousins" and "Grandparents" who served them and us during that difficult time.

Tribes work—be they the old-style or new models, where people truly care and reach out to serve and help. One friend knocked on our door one day as we were struggling with this, and boldly asked if I would show him my stack of bills. Unsure what he was up to, I took him to the room where my box of bills sat. He promptly put them all in his briefcase and refused to give them back to me. I was a little embarrassed and tried to talk him down, but he left, paid the bills, and never mentioned it again.

Another acquaintance, a tribe member who I didn't know very well, had spent months in a hospital with her own child and knew things others didn't. For example, she sent us phone cards, which surprised us until we learned that we couldn't use our cell phones in the hospital or use the hospital's lines to communicate. The phone cards were a miracle.

One of my wife's older sisters who lived a fair distance away, whom I had met on various occasions but didn't know very well in our Industrial world, moved in for a month and watched the kids and took care of everything. I came to consider her a dear friend. A family in our New Tribe education group noticed one of our sons was having a birthday (I had forgotten in the turmoil and Rachel was staying at the hospital) and threw him a huge birthday party with friends and presents and the whole works. There are so many other stories from this time.

Indeed, almost everybody who is connected to New Tribes can share similar experiences. This is the best of tribes, new or old. Working together on projects that matter, caring about each other and helping each other, and being there when the needs are the greatest; these are the mainstays of tribe. Speaking to the youth around the nation, it is clear to me that *e*-tribes are an emerging and important venue of friendship and connections.

Some find the superficiality of these connections a sticking point; others object to the waste of time connected to the electronic umbilicus; still others fret at the distance this accommodates in more central and present relationships of family and neighborhood. The Internet is at times uncivil, banal, and anti-social. While all of these are valid concerns, the fact of *e*-tribes is here, and I would assert that there are some important reasons for us to not only guard against the pitfalls, but also to fully embrace and expand on the good it can mean for our future.

I am hugely optimistic about the establishment of so many overlaying and intersecting networks of individuals who feel connected and loyal to one another, in spite of the diverse cultures, creeds, locations or lifestyles that they know. Such rapport and allegiance will hopefully facilitate the struggle to reweave our society's fabric of freedom and to overcome the threats of terrorism, economic disaster, issues of health, education, sustainable living, etc.

I look forward to the continued constructive discourse in the Great Conversation. The prospect of free exchange of information, ideas, and economic opportunity (and the liberating force that these are among populations where governmental oppression is a devastating fact of life) is cause for great hope. From micro lending to online instruction to family connections over long distances, the power for good is truly awe-inspiring.

Whether we speak of hunger, animal cruelty, moral degeneration in our inner cities, elder care, the decay of infrastructure, etc.: Whatever the societal ill, threat or problem, it can be powerfully impacted by creatively engaging the resources that today's technology affords us; and the greatest power online will be through, and as a result of, the establishment of tribal-type connections.

CHAPTER

21

Tribes, Nations, Civilizations and Mega-Cultures

It is likely that the New Tribes will have overlapping populations with nations for many decades to come. In fact, tribal thinking and structures already overlap with nations in most areas of the world. While international geo-politics is usually considered along the lines of nations and international organizations, in truth tribalistic worldviews now impact what happens in the world at the same or even higher levels than nations.

The most obvious examples of this are industrial-style tribes known as corporations and multi-national corporations. Other significant tribe-like institutions include religions, artistic and scientific and professional associations, family organizations, and many others. Some of these operate as New Tribes, while others follow older models of organization and interaction.

Civilizations

Samuel Huntington suggested that the world is increasingly divided into several large "civilizations" which are much bigger than most nations and which operate according to shared values and views of culture, history and ideals.[73] Such civilizations include Western Civilization (the U.S. and Europe), the Islamic world, Latin America, sub-Saharan Africa, Confucian culture, Russia, and others.

Like huge regional tribes, these civilizations are made up of various competing factions and usually see other civilizations as competitors or enemies. Indeed, the civilizations Huntington outlined had most of the problems of historical tribes with few of the benefits.

Huntington felt that civilizations would increasingly become more influential than nations in the 21st Century. Other experts such as Paul Kennedy, Francis Fukuyama, Jared Diamond, Alvin Toffler and Phillip Bobbitt have predicted that one way or another nations would become less and less dominant in the decades ahead.

Since Huntington shared his theories in the early and mid-1990s, trends have certainly shown the growing influence of civilizations. But we have also witnessed "mega-cultures" gaining even more influence than civilizations. Like the old tribes and modern national governments, civilizations are usually limited by geography. But the New Tribes and the post-modern mega-cultures usually connect virtually and are therefore not limited by geographical boundaries or restrictions.

Mega-Cultures

The major difference between civilizations and mega-cultures is this: People in a civilization share a common view of the past, agree on values, and share a common vision for the future, just like the old tribes. In contrast, the New Tribes and larger mega-cultures generally accept people from many diverse backgrounds, views and values, but cooperate and work together toward shared visions and goals for the future.

For example, in Western Civilization there is an ongoing and heated debate about the environment. Some passionately argue that global warming is a reality, while others vehemently deny the conclusiveness of the evidence. Politicians, scientists, journalists, pundits, researchers and marketers are brought into the battle.

But for the overwhelming majority of the population born after 1980, the debate is irrelevant. For them, environmentalism is a *value*. They couldn't care less what science proves about global warming or any other environmental debate. Regardless of the facts, they deeply *care* about the environment and value caring for it. They *believe* in using government policy to protect and benefit the environment. They ignore the debate because it has nothing to do with them—their values are set.

In a similar fashion, the Boomer generation still debates, discusses and even pontificates about gender issues, but those born after 1964 now deeply value gender equality. Whatever the Boomers say, it won't change this value. There are many similar examples, and they illustrate the significant differences between civilizations and mega-cultures.

Today there are at least five major mega-cultures in the world, large groups of people with a shared vision for the future and multiple institutions cooperating in attaining that vision. Each mega-culture is generally tribal in nature rather than nationalistic. Indeed, nations and national governments are typically sub-level institutions helping promote some of these mega-cultures.

Four of the five biggest mega-cultures are natural outgrowths of the 20th Century, the industrial age, and of mechanized-materialistic-national society. Still, each is increasingly adopting tribalistic features. Consider the following five major mega-cultures:

1. New Rome[74] is made up of many people in the United States, Canada, Europe, some in Japan, and a few others from around the world. New Rome envisions a future world increasingly run by the wealthy nations, with centralized national institutions and the masses ruled by a mix of the educated classes and advanced technology.

2. Masses Earth is a mega-culture made up of the large majority of the earth's human population, including most in Africa,

Latin America, Southeastern Asia and the masses in nearly all nations. This mega-culture is usually too busy just trying to survive to collaborate and envision a different future world. Members of Masses Earth want to feed themselves and their family and hopefully improve the prospects and opportunities for their children.

3. Phoenix Rising consists of a number of groups who want to re-gain world leadership or obtain it for the first time. There are several competing factions in this mega-culture, and they see all New Rome and the other Phoenix Rising factions as enemies in this process. The most powerful factions of this mega-culture are Russia, China, and Islamism. Significant parts of Latin America are also part of this wave.

4. The Electronic Herd[75] is less tied to national boundaries and citizenship than other people in the world, and members of this mega-culture want to influence the world toward higher levels of peace and cooperation while simultaneously increasing their own wealth.

Members of the Herd typically live in Mediterranean beach cities, bohemian American communities like those found in Ashland or Austin, Club Caribbean, or Cabinland (elite ranches in places like Montana or Sun Valley). Given modern technology, they are found almost everywhere.

Unlike the first three mega-cultures who count nations and governments among their support institutions, the Electronic Herd flows more from upper classes around the world than from national governments. Still, it is rooted in a natural class response to the mechanized-national world and its latest electronic and digital revolutions.

5. The New Tribes are a fifth growing mega-culture. Unlike the others, which are built around historical national and class models, the New Tribes are natural-born creations of the Information Age. They differ from the other four mega-cultures because they are truly a grass-roots phenomenon. They were

created by the little people, consist mostly of "regular" people, and are led by participants and thought leaders rather than officials, big investors, or any other type of superior.

There are also many more small factions within this group than in the other four. For example, New Rome is really one major faction, as is the Electronic Herd. Masses Earth is made up of many individuals, but there are few and perhaps no central institutions in this mega-culture—they are all part of the same faction. Even Phoenix Rising is made up of at most a few dozen major and minor factions.

But there are literally millions of New Tribes in the world, made up of many diverse people and seeking numerous goals and objectives. In many ways, the New Tribes may be the most potentially powerful of all groups in the world.

Most of these mega-cultures, like the New Tribes, are not re-stricted to any nation, social class or other confining demo-graphic, and they are growing in popularity and influence. Even where a faction within a mega-culture does generally coincide with a national government, such as in the cases of both Russia and China, the New Tribe dynamic is still showing itself to be increasingly inclusive and influential. Mega-cultures may even-tually even surpass the power of national governments—and in some ways already do.

The Diseases

Unfortunately, most of the mega-cultures are suffering from ma-jor diseases—though in truth, this is not always negative. Where the goals of a given mega-culture or faction are threats to free-dom, morality and prosperity, perhaps their illnesses are bless-ings in disguise.[76]

In any case, each of the mega-cultures has distinct and signifi-cant diseases. New Rome predictably suffers from Roman Dis-ease, and also has both Mandarin Disease and British Disease.

Roman Disease occurs where a nation cares more about money and entertainment than about virtue or freedom. In such a model, "bread and circuses" distract the people from facing and solving their national challenges. Rome burns while the people fiddle, because as long as they have food and entertainment they remain docile, self-centered and apathetic.

Mandarin Disease prioritizes social classes, status, experts, credentials and licensing over true quality, excellence, opportunity, initiative, innovation and achievement. As a result of Mandarin Disease, New Rome is upsizing government and downsizing small business, entrepreneurship and widespread leadership. The result of this choice in history has always reduced freedom and prosperity.

British Disease consists of increasing taxes and regulations in your own nation while spending more and more to maintain your empire or power abroad. This has caused the downfall of many great nations in history, and is a major problem for New Rome in our day.

Masses Earth is deeply sick and suffering from Sudan Disease. This condition occurs where outside help can't fix a depressed economy because aid and investment are consumed but not put to productive use. In societies with Sudan Disease, the lack of entrepreneurial initiative and ingenuity limits all progress.

Another illness ravaging Masses Earth is Chaos. More a syndrome than a disease, the lack of order, the rule of law or limits on government combine to create an environment where even entrepreneurial initiative and leadership are worthless because roaming armies, warlords, gangs and factions simply steal the fruits of any enterprise. Sudan Disease and Chaos reinforce each other in a vicious cycle of poverty, violence and misery.

Phoenix Rising has the illnesses of Spartan Disease and Utopian Disease. Spartan Disease is a mental illness that comes from a deep-seated though flawed belief in command economies, totalitarian politics and warlike expansion. Societies with Spartan

Disease are capable of accomplishing big projects and sometimes of militarily dominating free societies for a time, but eventually they turn on themselves because they believe in the lies of force, violence and abusive power. Societies with Spartan Disease consider freedom weak.

Note that when free societies allow themselves to be infected by Roman, Mandarin or British Disease, they sometimes lose to totalitarian societies. But it is the weaknesses of these diseases that make free nations vulnerable. Free societies that are healthy and free of these pathologies are usually invincible to outside attack.

Utopian Disease infects societies that arrogantly think they are ideal and therefore fail to openly listen to ideas and promote leaders from outside of official channels. When society shuts down initiative, stifles creativity, and opposes all but the established way of doing things (although the perception of this "long tradition" is usually at odds with history), there is little innovation and few leaders are created. Societies with Spartan Disease routinely suppress the most effective leaders and groups within their population and exacerbate Utopian Disease.

The Electronic Herd suffers from American Disease and also Greek Disease. American Disease is characterized by a belief in technology and economics over morality and principles. Greek Disease, based on the lessons of ancient Greek tribes, is a syndrome where the leaders are overwhelmed by a society's challenges and quietly give up. They make a separate peace with world events, quietly amassing personal wealth and estates (often in other countries) where they can weather national collapse if (or when) needed.

Instead of sacrificing all for their nation and people, they escape to safety or prepare escape plans even while the nation is collapsing. They don't mention this strategy to the masses, however, leaving regular citizens to suffer when the problems they were never warned about inevitably arrive. Conservative journalist Peggy Noonan recently warned that many American leaders are making a "separate peace" of this type today.[77]

Health Insurance

While specific New Tribes may suffer from these or other diseases, as a group the New Tribes are generally healthy and free of disease. The reason for this may simply be their youth. In contrast, the other four big mega-cultures are built on the national-materialistic society of the Industrial Age that is now increasingly elderly and infirm.

Another possible cause of New Tribe health is their openness and inclusiveness. America flourished while it followed the motto immortalized on the Statue of Liberty: "Give us your tired, your poor, your huddled masses…"[78] Today many New Tribes are accepting of all and are greatly benefiting from this diversity.

Another reason the New Tribes are flourishing is their freedom. They are hardly regulated, and even in the most totalitarian nations the New Tribes are among the least regulated groups due to their frequently virtual and non-geographical nature. Whatever the cause of the health and vibrancy of the New Tribes, they promise great hope for the future of freedom in the 21st Century.

Leadership in the New Tribes

But institutions rise no higher than their leaders, and the New Tribes need leadership just like any other group. On the positive side, the sheer number of New Tribes means that as they train leaders they significantly benefit the quantity of leaders in society. Of course, the quality of leadership is also vital to the future of freedom, prosperity and happiness.

The specific needs of leadership change over time, and are found in a combination of the great leadership lessons of the past and the greatest challenges of the present and near future. Mixing the wisdom of past tribes and other types of leadership with the needs of our century suggests that several key principles of leadership apply to the New Tribes.

Leaders of the New Tribes will gain much by considering and applying the following leadership suggestions:

1. **Be a leader**. Everyone is a leader in the New Tribes. In every tribe you belong to, you have the ability to share your views and leadership. Get involved. Participate. Don't take over, but don't just follow. Listen, consider, learn, discuss, consult, study, share and help contribute to meaningful discussions, debates, innovations and decisions. In short, you are needed as a leader.

2. **Be a change expert**. Learn to cultivate, study and become skilled at anticipating and leading change. Learn to help others change easily and effectively and flourish under new circumstances, environments and realities. Learn to truly *enjoy* the process of change.

3. **Be yourself.** Follow the age-old wisdom of the sages: Be yourself. The era of industrial-age management trained in assembly-line conformity is over. Since most of the current managers, and also many of the experts who train managers in the universities, were trained in the old conveyor-belt system, there is still huge pressure on leaders to be like everyone else. But this doesn't bring success in the new economy or the New Tribes.

   Marketing expert Seth Godin's advice to be a Purple Cow[79] is enlightening. Few people have seen a purple cow, so when they see one they stop and take a picture. *Then they tell everyone they know about it.*

   This is a parable for leadership in the new economy: Each of us is unique, an individual, with singular great talents to add to the world. Instead of trying to be like everyone else, we all need to embrace our inner purple cow and share with the world the great things only we can offer.

   The world desperately needs more leaders, and it needs the type of leader only you can be. It needs you to be you!

   Of course, we can all improve. Being ourselves isn't an excuse to be mediocre. It is a clarion call to be great, to become great in the way only you can be.

4. **Be a warrior!** Fight the right battle. Ask yourself what is needed, what you feel passionate about, and how can you make a positive difference in the world! This is an age of warriors, not salesmen.

Too many people haven't figured this out yet—they are still mentally caught in the nationalized, prosperous times before 9/11. They haven't realized yet that the world has changed and that we are in an era of tribal leadership and major challenges that will last for many years ahead.

Fight against the odds. Find and fight *your* battle. Be sure you are on the right side, and don't become smug, arrogant or self-righteous. Stay inclusive, tolerant, forgiving, positive and friendly. And with all this, find out what battles you were born to fight and go win them.

5. **Be wise.** Think, consider, analyze and take action. Don't be stymied by analysis, but do take the time to think things through, strategize and plan. Consult with other wise people in your life. Study and learn from history, the classics and any other source of wisdom. Be widely read and think deeply about what you read. Change your mind when you learn you have been wrong, and stick to the things you know to be true. Pay the price to be always learning.

6. **Be bold.** Take wise risks, be willing to make mistakes, and learn from your errors. The world needs to change, not stay the same, and that means that leaders must take action. When you know you are on the right course, boldly go forward.

Above all, be humble. Don't take yourself too seriously. Laugh a lot. Laugh at yourself. Face and overcome your weaknesses, and be patient with other people. Learn from everyone, and never consider yourself superior to anyone. And, when it is time to act, know that you are acting wisely. And be bold.

7. **Be optimistic.** Ours is an age where people fear, worry, stress and feel daily and even constant anxiety. The plague of our day is fear. Instead, trust! Relax. Believe that things will turn

out well. We all need to do our best, and we all need to do our part. But if we do our little portion of improving the world, that's all that is needed. Don't feel overwhelmed or incapable. Things will work out. They do, and they will.

A Time for Leaders

These things are central to leadership in the New Tribes, and they are foundational skills of leaders in the 21st Century. A century that began with 9/11 and jets flying into buildings clearly demands the highest caliber of leaders. Whatever challenges are ahead, the quality of our leadership will make all the difference.

Most importantly, our century requires that nearly all of us become leaders. We need the type of leadership education gained from the classics, entrepreneurial experiences, independent thinking and active political involvement. We need a society of leaders who build and lead the New Tribes in all arenas of life— toward greater freedom and prosperity.

The great need, and challenge, of our times is to pass this kind of leadership and the society it will create to our children and grandchildren. This is our time, and it is a time for leadership. The future of freedom, prosperity, family and happiness hang in the balance....

The Eight Meanings of Freedom

A new tribe is needed. Actually, its constituents have been around for a long time. But they have functioned as individuals, sometimes as families, and more rarely as small groups of people. But as a tribe or nation, they have never gained traction or achieved critical mass.

Such a tribe believes in freedom, real freedom, for all people in an ordered society that protects liberty for everyone. This ideal has been proposed by many, and fully achieved by no generation in history.

Two types of tribes—political parties and religious groups—have existed throughout the history of human tribes. Political parties originally grew out of the perpetual conflict between the rich and the poor, but over time parties in all nations have focused more on mere winning than promoting the content of their ideals. Freedom has tended to occur only when citizens look beyond parties and work together with all people who support freedom—regardless of party histories and passions.

Likewise, religious sentiment is one of the most powerfully animating and unifying of forces toward tribal community—both for good and for ill (often within the same nominal tribe). It is unfortunate that some people of the purest faith and the most deeply held convictions about peace, charity, freedom, family, etc., seem to have little ability to connect with anyone but those who already share their views—from Judeo-Christian to Ethical Secularist. I think this limits their influence for good; and in most cases, I don't see that the actual doctrines of their faith require this sort of isolationism, but rather idealize just the opposite.

For an effective freedom tribe to exist, many citizens must get past the natural human tendency to isolate ourselves in cocoons of people who agree with us. Freedom only comes when people of differing views work together on the common goal of liberty. No Freedom*Shift* is possible without this.

False Two's

Three of the biggest challenges of our time—the need for a revolution of entrepreneurship, the need for more independent-thinking citizens, and the need for more leadership in the emerging *e*-tribes and other new-style tribal groups of the world—all unite in their call for the growth of a new tribe dedicated to freedom.

Author John Anthony West wrote, "The degree to which one understands 'Three' is a fair indication of the degree to which he or she is civilized."[80] In other words, the tendency for rigid binary thought, regardless of the level of technology or complexity a society may possess, is a fair indication that it is actually either relatively backward in nature, or degenerating as a society. And the dialectical ability to look beyond the obvious two presenting choices is the essence of enlightenment and true leadership.

One of the major reasons the tribe of freedom has seldom achieved power in the world is that human beings naturally tend to break into competing groups—but without dividing on the *true* lines of difference. Madison outlined the benefits of this tendency in Federalist 10, and there are many positives of factionalism that have contributed to American freedom. But there is also a major downside.

Tocqueville taught in *Democracy in America* that every nation divides itself into two major parties, each competing with the other for ascendancy. He called these the party of aristocracy and the party of democracy—one seeking to divide the people according to class, and the other attempting to spread freedom and opportunity for all.

In America these became the party of agriculture *versus* industry, then North *versus* South, later the city *versus* the country, and most recently Democrats *versus* Republicans. But dividing the nation into red and blue states (or liberal coasts *versus* conservative flyover states) misses the real division among us. Ancient divisions between aristocrats and peasants, as well as medieval conflicts between feudal lords and neighboring states, made the same mistake. When war arose in history, re-alignment into Hawks and Doves also missed the point. So did historical conflicts over the color of roses and violent arguments between religions.

Our historical and modern divisions are not the real divisions, and this means that the battles go on for all of history without conclusion or solution. To end the conflicts, to fix the unending battling of sides, we need to clearly understand the two sides as they really are—the real parties.

The Real Divide

Unlike elementary or high school culture, and unlike college, career and even adult culture, the real divide takes us all the way back to kindergarten. Indeed it is one of those key lessons that we all should have learned in early childhood. In some ways (as humorously recounted by author Robert Fulghum), the lessons of kindergarten are the most important of all.

The divide in political discourse (and in much of human relations) can be analyzed with a basic criterion: Some people spend their lives angry and afraid, while others live in the attitudes of hopeful and helpful. These emotional postures form the basis of a real-world philosophical schism.

Angry and Afraid

The Scarcity Party sees a world of battling, competition, scarcity, winning or losing, and always trying to get ahead. Its members see others as either potential mates or potential enemies. They quickly notice differences between people, and they seek to get themselves and those in their group (family, race, religion, faction, nation, etc.) ahead of everyone else. They want others to lose more, and for their own to win more.

In their anger and fear, they avoid pain, push for whatever they think will benefit them, and are willing to step on others to get what they want. The Angry & Afraid Scarcity Party (A^2) has a long and sad history of causing, escalating and reliving most of the problems in world history. They are the Manipulators and Destroyers.

Hopeful and Helpful

In contrast, the Hopeful & Helpful members of the Abundance Party (H^2) spend their lives trying to help people, improve themselves, and seek better lives and a better world. Because they are not afraid, it is fine with them if others don't support them or do something different. They are secure.

For the Abundance Party, life is not about themselves. Yes, it is about becoming better; but even this goal is a means to helping the world improve. If they were angry, they would expect everyone else to join them in fixing the world, and even try to use the force of government to require charity. But they are content to do their own work of improving the world and helping others, inspiring and urging them to be and do their best through exemplary leadership, rather than expend angry energy trying to force others to change.

Pretty much every nation, organization, philosophy, political viewpoint, religion, community, and company has both A^2s and also H^2s. The H^2 Partiers do nearly all of the good in these groups, while the A^2s cause nearly all of the problems.

If the H^2s from all groups would work together, the mischief of the A^2s would soon be mitigated. But as it is, the H^2s constantly find themselves in superficially adversarial positions from each other (due to their institutional affiliations) even though such conflict is not their purpose or their nature.

Ironically, if you have strong Democratic ties it is tempting to call Democrats the Hopeful & Helpful and label Republicans the Angry & Afraid; those with loyal Republican connections assign the opposite labels. But neither type of labeling is truly accurate. There are a lot of H^2s and A^2s in both major political parties.

The H^2s and the A^2s make up most of the members of the Democrats, Republicans, independents, socialists, environmentalists, right-wingers, radical leftists and every other political group. If you know what to look for, they are pretty easy to recognize. The A^2s include those who are any of the following: Bush-haters, Obama-loathers, racists, bigoted about religious or secular beliefs, promoters of violence in modern America, etc.

Republicans like to point out the Angry & Afraid people in the Democratic Party and act as if they speak for the whole party, and the Democrats do the same thing when attacking Republicans.

An interesting hybrid also exists, which is likewise problematic. Historically, too many Democrats have combined *Afraid and Helpful*, while too often Republicans have been *Angry and Hopeful*. Unfortunately, the internal conflict and the philosophical and operational inconsistencies of these amalgams basically cancel out the good they could do to truly promote freedom and make a difference for good.

The world needs more hopeful and helpful people, and the future of our freedom and prosperity depends on it. The strong emotions of anger and fear too frequently block the path to progress. However, before we can fully understand the differences between these two major Parties of the A^2s and the H^2s, and the application of this construct, we need to understand the eight meanings of freedom.

Eight is Enough

There are six great basic traditions of freedom, each enjoying differing levels of support from various political and social groups. These include political freedom, economic freedom, religious freedom, individual freedoms (often called privacy), freedom of the press, and academic freedom (sometimes called freedom of thought).

The seventh and eighth freedoms are actually forms of protection. A seventh freedom, national security, consists of using power to defend these other freedoms from aggressors and attackers. And social justice, an eighth freedom, is the process of ensuring that these other freedoms are truly available to all people—not just to a limited few from a certain class, race, or other group.

A few leftist radicals use "social justice" to mean the extreme redistribution of wealth from rich to poor in socialistic and even communistically controlling ways; just as fringe right wingers at times promote almost-fascist government powers in the name of "national security." However, the more reasonable and normal definition of social justice (and national security) is essential to freedom: to take constitutional freedoms to all.

True liberty requires all eight types of freedom. Anything less falls short (although any measure of freedom is certainly better than none). Indeed, a society that increases one of these freedoms is nearly always headed in the right direction. And, in fact, each freedom tends to promote the adoption of the other seven. For example, increased academic freedom or freedom of the press naturally encourages the spread of political and economic freedoms—and vice versa. Freedom promotes freedom, just as force encourages the increase of force.

Unfortunately, the historical reality is that the two major American political ideologies have tended to emphasize the following division:

Conservative	Liberal
political freedoms	individual freedoms (privacy)
economic freedoms	freedom of the press
religious freedoms	academic freedom
national security	social justice

Fighting each other over which column is most important is misguided and dangerous. It has seldom brought anything but pain to our nation and its citizens. This becomes even clearer when we consider the focus of the Scarcity Party from both the conservative and liberal camps: "Stop the extremists on the other side from taking away our freedoms in the name of their petty and radical pet projects."

Such a view is highly inaccurate, and comes from fear, anger and a deep lack of trust. While it is true that the Angry & Afraid types within the other Party will continue to cause negatives, it is more important to notice that the Helpful & Hopeful folks on the other side are truly trying to make the world better.

Whatever you may think about the "other" party, an important segment of both Republicans and Democrats are actually H^2. Many independents and entrepreneurs are naturally inclined to the H^2 perspective. As more people think about politics in a nonpartisan and increasingly independent way, and as more people become entrepreneurs and develop leadership skills like greatly increased initiative and tenacity and so forth, the H^2 viewpoint will continue to spread.

Unfortunately, in politics, Republicans and Democrats often vehemently promote the four freedoms they value most and simultaneously discount or attack the other four. Other parties and many independents make the same mistake. For example, some conservatives frequently denigrate the freedoms of privacy or the press in their attempts to promote religion, while some liberals too often trample economic or political freedoms in their zeal to increase social justice.

Likewise, conservatives sometimes deny social justice when political and economic freedoms are not really at stake, just like liberals at times refuse to allow religious freedom or incentivize the power of the private sector out of fear that social justice must be an exclusively government project. Both sides engage battles for their pet types of freedom, and then don't turn off the fight even when the other side suggests something truly positive.

Kindergarten Lessons

All of this is the natural result of the Angry & Afraid worldview. In reality, the Hopeful & Helpful people in both the Democratic and Republican Parties, as well as the H^2 independents and members of minor parties, really do care about all eight freedoms. Some have been inclined to focus on certain freedoms above others, either by their upbringing, education or party affiliations, but those with an H^2 outlook are friends of all eight freedoms.

When we start to comprehend this more accurate view of the world, a new understanding of the real division emerges.

The chart on the next page is remarkably different than the one we saw earlier, and it illuminates the major difference between the fundamental values and attitudes of the two real parties—the A^2 and the H^2. Their views of the past, current issues, and visions for the future could hardly be more divergent.

Both groups of course include pessimistic and also idealist people, and there are various different schools of thought in both. But the most significant factor separating these two great Parties of humanity is their worldview. The Hopeful & Helpfuls value their own ability to contribute to the world, while the Angry & Afraids see themselves as victims of a powerful "they" which is to be opposed, feared and hated.

The H^2s see that all six of the basic freedoms are vital, that social justice spreads these six freedoms, and that national security protects and maintains them. Together, all eight freedoms are essential for a healthy, free and prosperous society.

Scarcity Party	Abundance Party
political freedoms for me and mine	political freedoms for all, everywhere
economic freedoms for me and mine	economic freedoms for all, everywhere
religious freedom for me and mine	religious freedom for all, toleration, open mindedness
individual freedoms for me	individual freedoms for all, everywhere
freedom to say what I want	freedoms of expression and the press
freedom to think what I want	academic freedom for all, celebration of many views
national security	national security for all nations
victory for me and mine	social justice for all peoples

The Freedom Tribe

Our nation and world desperately needs a Party of Freedom. Such a party would not be an official political party, since its goal would be to unite and build rather than to win or govern. It would be made up of everyone who believes in all eight facets of freedom, and that we can work together to promote them, increase and spread them, and keep them protected and safe in a dangerous world. It would be full of people who approach the world in an attitude of hope and help.

The idea of a freedom party is made realistic by the technology of the day, which allows people from all places and walks of life to connect and cooperate. Such a party would have a higher-than-usual makeup of entrepreneurs, and many creeds and backgrounds. The one thing they would share in common is a belief in the essential value of all eight meanings of freedom.

Certainly such a tribe would have its share of debates, factions, and disagreements, all of which are healthy to freedom. The guiding value would be that any proposal, policy or plan they supported would be good for freedom overall—not just good for one type of freedom at the cost of another.

We need a freedom party in our day, an unofficial tribe of people working together on the shared vision of more freedom for all people in each nation of the world. Of course, given the reality of our modern world, such a party does not need to be a single, organized entity with bylaws and officers. In fact, freedom will benefit most if many people simply promote the eight types of freedom in the organizations and groups they already support.

For freedom to truly increase and flourish, it needs to become more of a value to all of us. We need the following:

- An informal freedom party made up of many diverse people and tribes that share the philosophy of full freedom with all the other groups and peoples

- An understanding that when we promote one type of freedom at the expense of another we actually hurt us all

- A commitment to more openly look beyond our own limited opinions and cooperate with people of differing views who truly do care about freedom

Without all of these, freedom will struggle and decline. For those who love freedom, it is time to broaden and deepen our understanding of true freedom. It is time to use our influence to spread the values and ideas of freedom. The technology is there, and it is time to use it. Real freedom has always been a bottom-up project led by the regular people in a society. All eight facets of freedom are essential, and it is up to the regular people to promote them all. This is the future of freedom, and it depends on each of us.

As we consider our alliances, affiliations and tribes, we must bear in mind that in virtually every camp, and bearing every label, there are those who prefer to shout about it and those who prefer to do something about it. Those who love freedom can no longer avoid potential alliances because of differences in political affiliations, religious beliefs, differences between believers and secularists, labor and management, gender or ethnic differences, or other factions that hinder our success toward the common goal.

Any serious movement to establish and ensure freedom and prosperity for the generations to come will be critically understaffed and fatally fractured if—simply because they are significantly different from us in some way—we fail to build alliances with others who are earnest and willing to work toward common ideals.

Who Can Stand

Today, as we begin to see the unraveling of what has been, the message of warning and the sentiment of the inevitability of change seem alarmist and extreme to some; but I believe that the time for false optimism is past. It falls to us now to join ranks with those who understand our place in history to answer the call and use the remaining months and years of security to prepare for what will surely be.

I do not know what shape our generation's challenges will take, but the daily news suggests many plausible forms: economic collapse, catastrophic violence, threats to our food supply, pandemics and plagues, the rapid and drastic alteration of constitutional forms and protections—or the likely combination of many of these factors. Just imagine the impact of a major e-virus, or an electromagnetic pulse that fry any unprotected electrical circuitry—from your watch and your car to the trains, planes and trucks that make the country run, to the power grid and cellular networks, etc. (Knock on wood.) Challenges will come—in some form or another.

I assert that God's miraculous power delivered those rag-tag

American revolutionaries from challenges at least as great as the ones we face. And while there are many in our generation who may be their equals in terms of scholarly understanding, perhaps we have yet to prove that our character is sufficient to merit the intervention of Providence. True, many are well educated in the proper role of government, are well-practiced in dealing with crises and challenges, are gifted in leading, teaching, serving and inspiring. And for all the good they are capable of due to these attributes and this consecrated preparation, the greatest threat still lies within.

We must surrender our personal weaknesses, insecurities and pride. We must celebrate the best effort of every man or woman, no matter what else we may disagree upon; we must learn to recognize allies in strange places, and set aside differences that render such alliances ineffective.

During the Good Times of the 1980s and 1990s it was critical that we diligently worked to define our cultural ideals and that our education and efforts were in harmony with those ideals. It brings to mind the epoch of Biblical history in which the Good Times prophet Isaiah was so vehemently opposed to the incursion of Babylonian values into the Israelite nation. And yet, as the cycles turned, the Crisis prophet Jeremiah spoke boldly for a new policy of tolerance and friendship. This was not a repudiation of Isaiah; both were right *for their time*. I believe we should consider how this applies to us today.

Jesus of Nazareth crossed the societal lines of religion, principle, decorum and propriety to move the cause of liberty and to inspire greatness in the leper, the tax collector, the prostitute and the Pharisee (in Nicodemus and Joseph of Arimathea). In every conceivable way he modeled for us that there is a time to take the hand of all allies from all backgrounds.

Would you win the battle for freedom? Then consider this challenge. Who is your nominal "enemy"? If it can be said of him that he loves freedom and family, be an asset in his effort to achieve his worthy goals. Be a model of peaceful conduct, of fearless friendship. Make him your ally. Or at least be his ally. The tyranny of aristocracy will not rest lighter upon our children because of our unyielding narrow-minded loyalty to lesser objectives and affiliations in the battle against it. Our only hope to turn back the tide already too far gone is to have no other object in mind than this.

We must model virtue, wisdom, diplomacy and courage. We must lay aside *our* pride and bring down *our* walls. We must link arms with any who is willing to make a gain on any front against the loss of freedom. We will hope in vain for an ideological army large enough that consists solely of those who agree with us on all points. Such zealous crusades may win many skirmishes, but will likely find that in so doing we neglected to counter the advances of the greater enemy, and will ultimately lose the war.

It is time to re-examine our assumptions and our definitions, even *as* we take a stand. Upon challenging our own assumptions, we find adequate justification for granting to others the latitude of their own conscience, and the ability to agree to disagree on some things as we stand firm together on others.

There are many levels on which we must improve. Too few of us are prepared to give a persuasive voice for the protection of life, liberty and property, and we "persuade" only those who already agree with us.

I believe freedom *will* win. The battle now is, as it always has been, a battle for men's hearts and souls, one by one. We must each look within to ensure that our hearts are whole, and then seek to win allies not by shouting them down, marginalizing them or overpowering their minds or their wills, but by entreating their hearts with honest friendship. This is the true triumph of the Freedom's Tribe, and our only hope for victory.

A Decision

> **Will we adopt The Three Choices?**
> **If not, freedom will consistently decrease until it is entirely lost.**
> **We are making the decision right now, whether we know it or not.**

Great progress is always the result of small and simple ideas whose time has come. We need a Freedom*Shift* in our world, and we need it soon. While America and the world face many problems and challenges, three small solutions will change everything:

- First, a resurrection of the entrepreneurial mindset will free up genius, initiative, innovation, leadership and ingenuity.

- Second, a rebirth of active citizen involvement in government—both within and outside of the parties—will drastically spread the principles and practices of freedom.

- Third, opening our minds to the lessons of traditional tribes and applying them to the emerging power of New Tribes will increase thinking, incentive, entrepreneurship and prosperity.

The result of these three small changes will revolutionize America and the world—peacefully, prosperously and progressively. The new millennium was born in travail and pain on September 11 of its opening year, 2001, and it is now struggling to come of age. The clarion call of this new millennium is this: To bring back the great ideal of freedom in better, enhanced, inclusive and improved ways in our time.

Freedom has been the greatest earthly quest of humanity—its families, governments, businesses, churches, communities, media, art, science and many other endeavors. The epic journey of every man and woman of this earth, the work and sacrifice through many generations and spanning the entire globe, is the search for real and lasting freedom. It is what our ancestors lived for and what our posterity will most prize.

Of course, when freedom is achieved, humanity seeks other things as well. But without freedom, the other pursuits of happiness are stifled and blocked. Freedom is necessary for true morality, prosperity and progress. When freedom is in peril, a Freedom*Shift* is needed to promote the principles of freedom in many facets of society. Will we be that Freedom Shift?

If this feels overstated or cliché, simply turn to the pages of history, or the current media around the world. No pursuit is older, more challenging, or more natural than the cause of liberty. Business puts economic freedom above all things, just like churches value religious freedom, media values freedom of the press, professors value academic freedom, and even branches of government prize judicial or executive or legislative independence. Levels of government likewise value their autonomy above all things.

Sometimes the word "freedom" has been used as license for one group to abuse, enslave or otherwise fall short of its potential. But these are the counterfeit, not the reality of freedom.

Freedom is man's greatest ambition, rarest achievement and continuing ideal. In literature, no theme is more prevalent than freedom in its various forms—from freedom within marriage to over-dominant families to man's perpetual quest for more independence. In our day, thanks to the age of information, it has never been so simple to learn about freedom. But without The Three Choices, such learning will be shallow and unimpactful.

The Three Choices will empower our generation to effectively meet its challenges. The Three will boost us to an entirely new level.

The Three Choices go beyond learning, though they start with learning. Once we truly learn our role, we must take action to build businesses, innovate, independently impact freedom, and cooperate with others to improve the world. We can read a classic, start a business, deeply study an issue, join or start a New Tribe. In a thousand ways we can make a positive difference. We can, and we must.

Freedom requires people who are capable of freedom, and one thing The Three Choices all have in common is that they are the result of people using their will to take initiative and action in the world. More is happening than the media tell us.

Who will implement The Three Choices? Who will take them to the world and establish them at all levels of society? Only a relatively few people are needed, in comparison to the millions of Americans and billions who live on the earth.

At least three types of people are needed. Without them, The Three Choices will not be adopted. With them, The Three Choices will help change the future of freedom, prosperity and the pursuit of happiness.

The first type reads and thinks widely and deeply, and understands the principles of freedom upon which societal success depends. It closely watches society and makes its influence felt wherever the need arises. We call this group Producer-Citizens.

The second type builds entrepreneurial ventures and helps spread freedom in society by creating prosperity and spreading the values of initiative, innovation and tenacity. We call this group Social Leaders.

The third type understands the principles of freedom deeply, at the levels of Thomas Jefferson and the greatest leaders and statesmen of history. They dedicate much of their lives to studying freedom in great depth and detail. This group is the Statesmen.

Producer-Citizens, Social Leaders, Statesmen. All three are needed. I challenge every reader to become one of these three types of leaders. (A free action guide for this is found in the white paper from our think tank, The Center for Social Leadership, entitled: "Reweaving the Fabric of Freedom." Available for pdf download at www.thesocialleader.com.)

The Three Choices may well matter as much to our generation as getting on the ark did in Noah's time. I do not think this is an exaggeration. The literal future of freedom and prosperity is at stake. A great Freedom*Shift* is needed.

Of course there will still be challenges to overcome even once our society has adopted The Three Choices. But one thing is certain: Without The Three Choices, *freedom will decrease*. Without a Freedom*Shift* in our day, the future of freedom is bleak.

But I am an optimist; I am confident that the necessary Freedom*Shift* will come. Indeed it has already begun. It is time for each of us to join those who are promoting freedom around the world. It is time for each of us to ask, "If our freedoms are lost, what else matters? How can I make a difference? Where should I start?" The answers to such questions are the spark of freedom. Freedom starts small, and then it grows. But we can never grow complacent and depend on the freedom of the past. Freedom must begin anew with each cycle of history, and now is the time for our Freedom Shift.

The Three Choices Have Worked Before

Perhaps no recent or historical example of reweaving the fabric of freedom has more to teach us than that of India's successful quest for independence, as led by Mohandas Gandhi. In his peaceful crusade to liberate his homeland from not only the colonization of the British imperialists but from the grip of cultural decay, Gandhi went to great lengths to establish The Three Choices among his people.

He sought a **return to tribal ideals** as he praised the simple life; and he set a personal example by his vegetarian lifestyle, natural healing and hygiene. *Gram swaraj*, or village self-rule, was central to his vision for the ideal societal model.

He urged people to **think creatively and independently**, to look beyond the accepted norms of rigid castes and to reject traditional means of violence and hatred as the tools of their revolution. Virtually every policy and utterance was a plea to consider a different option than the obvious ones that the two sides of the controversy might promote.

He admonished his people to **embrace the values of entrepreneurship** and chose the spinning wheel to be a symbol of this way of life. He urged the Indians to create a cottage industry by spinning and weaving their own cloth—thereby taking on the struggle against the textile industry of England. He even gave public lectures with his "charkha," or spinning wheel, set before him as the icon of freedom, self-reliance and tribal identity.

The story of India's ascendency is the story of The Three Choices being put into practice.

The Value of One Thread

With each life, each thread,[81] each choice, each principle, woven into the grand design, we will see not just the renaissance of freedom in our communities, but the hope for liberty for all peoples around the world restored. Have we grown too sophisticated for such idealism? I dearly hope not.

The principles of the U.S. Constitution light the way, as do the contributions of all great women and men who stood up for freedom.

While The Three Choices are simple, it will not be easy to implement them throughout our society. We have gone in the opposite direction now for many decades. But the future of freedom is at stake; without The Three Choices our freedoms will consistently decrease. We've been without serious threats for so long that we do not realize the cost of the freedom we take for granted. If we do not choose to act now to preserve it, we can expect the price to regain it to be far higher in the future. It was Thomas Paine who said:

> What we obtain too cheap, we esteem too lightly. Heaven knows how to put a proper price upon its goods; and it would be strange indeed, if so celestial an article as Freedom should not be highly rated.[82]

The longer we wait, the more difficult it will be for future generations to apply The Three Choices and re-energize freedom. A powerful Freedom*Shift* is needed, a drastic change in the level and direction of our freedom. When a Freedom*Shift* occurs, many institutions and ideas that have tended to rely on force and build controls will switch to supporting the principles of freedom. We need such a Freedom*Shift* in our day.

As noted before: Such major shifts are usually caused by surprisingly small and simple things that make all the difference. The Three Choices are such things, and they carry incredible potential power. Yes, it is a daunting task; and like every Freedom *Shift* generation, we must ask ourselves the question: *What is the alternative?*

We have the mettle to succeed, and it is time to get started.

NOTES

1. See The Institute for Intercultural Studies, FAQ about Mead/Batesman.

2. See *The Political Writings of John Adams*, "Letters to John Taylor, of Caroline, Virginia"; edited by George W. Carey. Regnery Publishing, Inc., 2000.

3. See Great Books of the Western World, edited by Mortimer Adler.

4. See Henry David Thoreau, *Walden*.

5. See Robert Kiyosaki, *Rich Dad, Poor Dad* and *The Cashflow Quadrant*.

6. Thomas L. Friedman, "Start-Ups, Not Bailouts," *The New York Times*, April 4, 2010.

7. For more on Georgics and freedom, visit www.fourlostamericanideals.com.

8. See Andrew B. Wilson, "In Defense of Downsizing," *The Weekly Standard*, March 15, 2010.

9. See Strauss and Howe, The Fourth Turning.

10. See the writings of Clayton Christensen.

11. See Harriet Rubin, "CEO Libraries Reveal Keys to Success," *The New York Times*, July 27, 2007.

12. See Malcolm Gladwell, *Outliers*.

13. See, for example, Thomas Friedman, "Dreaming the Possible Dream," *The New York Times*, March 7, 2010.

14. See Jaron Lanier, "The serfdom of crowds," *Harper's Magazine*, February 2010 issue.

15. See Daniel Coyle, *The Talent Code*.

16. For more information, visit www.tjed.org.

17. See James Fallows, "Cyber Warriors," *The Atlantic*, March 2010. See Israel on its Internet Fighting Team in Harper's Index, *Harpers Magazine*, November 2009.

18. See David Brooks, "Patio Man and the Sprawl People," *The Weekly Standard*, August 12/August 19, 2002.

19. Quoted in David E. Sanger, "Deficits May Alter U. S. Politics and Global Power," *The New York Times*, February 1, 2010.

20. "Red Mist: China's Financial System," *The Economist*, February 6, 2010.

21. "Red Mist: China's Financial System," *The Economist*, February 6, 2010.

22. "Tougher and Tougher," *The Economist*, February 13, 2010. See also "China's National People's Congress," *The Economist*, February 27, 2010.

23. Howard W. French, "The Next Empire?" *The Atlantic*, May 2010.

24. See David Jolly and Catherine Rampell, "Moody's Says U.S. Debt Could Test Triple-A Rating," *The New York Times,* March 15, 2010.

25. "Briefing: Europe's Financial Crisis," *The Economist,* February 13, 2010.

26. Peggy Noonan, "Can Washington Cut Spending,?" *The Wall Street Journal*, February 20, 2010.

27. Ken Kurson, "A Hedge Fund for Little Guys," *Esquire,* March 2010; Michael Kinsley, "My Inflation Nightmare," *The Atlantic,* April 2010.

28. "Harper's Index," *Harper's Magazine,* March 2010.

29. Peggy Noonan, "Can Washington Cut Spending?," *The Wall Street Journal*, February 20, 2010.

30. "Clash of Generations," a review of *The Pinch: How the Baby Boomers Took their Children's Future—and Why They Should Give it Back,* by David Willetts, *The Economist,* February 13, 2010.

31. See Robert Fulghum, *Everything I Really Need to Know, I Learned in Kindergarten.*

32. Jean Twenge, quoted in Don Peck, "How a New Jobless Era Will Transform America," *The Atlantic,* March 2010.

33. Ron Aslop, quoted in Don Peck, "How a New Jobless Era Will Transform America," *The Atlantic,* March 2010.

34. Larry Druckenbrod, quoted in Don Peck, "How a New Jobless Era Will Transform America," *The Atlantic,* March 2010.

35. Don Peck, "How a New Jobless Era Will Transform America," *The Atlantic,* March 2010.

36. "The Net Generation, Unplugged," *The Economist,* March 6, 2010.

37. Matthew Continetti, "Not the One They Were Hoping For," *The Weekly Standard*, March 8, 2010.

38. "The Net Generation, Unplugged," *The Economist,* March 6, 2010.

39. "The Net Generation, Unplugged," *The Economist,* March 6, 2010.

40. See Matthew Continetti, "Not the One They Were Hoping For," *The Weekly Standard*, March 8, 2010.

41. Don Peck, "How a New Jobless Era Will Transform America," *The Atlantic,* March 2010.

42. See William Strauss and Neil Howe, *The Millennials.*

43. See William Strauss and Neil Howe, *The Millennials.*

44. CNN Live, March 10, 2010.

45. CNN Live, March 10, 2010.

46. "Sharing the Pain," *The Economist,* March 6, 2010.

47. Quoted in Thomas Friedman, "A Word From the Wise," *The New York Times,* March 3, 2010.

48. Quoted in Thomas Friedman, "A Word From the Wise," *The New York Times,* March 3, 2010.

49. Thomas Friedman, "A Word From the Wise," *The New York Times,* March 3, 2010.

50. See Oliver DeMille, *The Coming Aristocracy: Education and the Future of Freedom;* www.thecomingaristocracy.com.

51. See John Maynard Keynes, *The End of Laissez Faire.*

52. See David Brooks, "The Obama Slide," *The New York Times,* August 31, 2009.

53. See the writings of Ken Kurson.

54. Thomas L. Friedman, "Is China the Next Enron?" *The New York Times,* January 13, 2010.

55. David Brooks, "The Tel Aviv Cluster," *The New York Times,* January 12, 2010.

56. See *The Lexus and the Olive Tree, Bobos in Paradise, On Paradise Drive,* and others.

57. See V. I. Lenin, *Class Society and the State.*

58. Many of the ideas in this section come from John Maynard Keynes, *The End of Laissez Faire.*

59. Cited in Kevin Baker, "The Vanishing Liberal," *Harper's Magazine,* April 2010.

60. See, for example, Kevin Baker, "The Vanishing Liberal," *Harper's Magazine,* April 2010.

61. For a good commentary on these movements, from a liberal perspective, see Kevin Baker, "The Vanishing Liberal," *Harper's Magazine,* April 2010.

62. See Alexis de Tocqueville, *Democracy in America,* Volume I, chapters 1-5.

63. See Ken Wilber, *A Brief History of Everything* for many of the ideas in this section.

64. See Brant Secunda and Mark Allen, *Fit Soul, Fit Body.*

65. See the Dalai Lama, *The Art of Happiness.*

66. See Yogananda, *Autobiography of a Yogi.*

67. "While we pursue happiness, we flee from contentment." – Hasidic Proverb

68. See Virgil, *Georgics.*

69. See Marcus Aurelius, *Meditations.*

70. See 2 Chronicles 32:7.

71. See Oliver and Rachel DeMille, *Leadership Education: The Phases of Learning* for more on how to adopt tribal values in the home environment, within an extended family and in a community of neighbors.

72. Jason Lanier, "The Serfdom of Crowds," *Harper's Magazine,* February 2010.

73. See Samuel Huntington, *The Clash of Civilizations.*

74. The names of the mega-cultures and diseases are mine, with the exception of the Electronic Herd.

75. This phrase was coined by Thomas L. Friedman.

76. Special thanks to Dr. Brad Bolon for his help in developing these concepts.

77. Peggy Noonan, "A Separate Peace," *The Wall Street Journal*, October 27, 2005.

78. From "The New Colossus" by Emma Lazarus.

79. See Seth Godin, *Purple Cow, New Edition: Transform Your Business by Being Remarkable.*

80. See John Anthony West, *Serpent in the Sky: The High Wisdom of Ancient Egypt.*

81. As we undertake to reweave the fabric of freedom, the account of another weaver from fiction comes to mind:

    "…'the story is that we go to the place where the threads come from.'
    " 'What do you do there?'
    " 'We spin.'

    "Alvin tried to imagine Becca's mother, and her grandmother, and the women before that, all in a line, he tried to imagine how many there'd be, all of them working their spinning wheels, winding out threads from the spindle, yarn all raw and white, which would just go somewhere, go on and disappear somewhere until it broke. Or maybe when it broke they held the whole thing, a whole human life, in their hands, and then tossed it upward until it was caught by a passing wind, and then dropped down and then got caught up in somebody's loom. A life afloat on the wind, then caught and woven into the cloth of humanity; born at some arbitrary time, then struggling to find its way into the fabric, weaving into the strength of it.

    "And as he imagined this, he also imagined that he understood something about that fabric. About the way it grew stronger the more tightly woven in each thread became. The ones that skipped about over the top of the cloth, dipping into the weft only now and then, they added little to the strength, though much to the color, of the cloth. While some whose color hardly showed at all, they were deeply wound among the threads, holding all together. There was a goodness in those hidden binding threads. Forever from then on, Alvin would see some quiet man or woman, little noticed and hardly thought of by others, who nevertheless went a-weaving through the life of village, town, or city, binding up, holding on, and Alvin would silently salute such folk, and do them homage in his heart, because he knew how their lives kept the cloth strong, the weave tight." Orson Scott Card, *The Red Prophet.*

82. See Thomas Paine, *The Crisis.*

WORKS BY OLIVER DEMILLE

Audio Presentations

The Four Lost American Ideals

The Freedom Crisis

The Great Depression of 2012

The 7 Keys of Great Teaching

Worldviews and the Emerging State

Cycles from the Classics

A Thomas Jefferson Education Audio Book

For more information on these titles, visit:

http://tjed.org/purchase/audio-downloads/

Connect with Oliver DeMille:

Visit TJEd.Org or OliverDeMille.com for more by Oliver DeMille

Thomas Jefferson Education for Teens
(with Shanon Brooks)

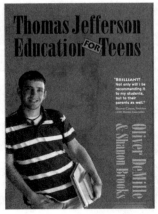

This latest addition to the TJEd library is written to youth and adults wanting to accomplish a successful Scholar Phase—academics, personal development and mission preparation.

From the Introduction:

"It is said that when God wants to change the world, he sends a baby—perfectly timed to grow, learn, prepare and then take action at the right moment. But there are times when one baby won't suffice, when the challenges facing the world are just too great; and so instead of a great reformer or a few key thinkers, what is needed is a whole generation of leaders. This happened in the sixth century B.C. and in the first decade of the Common Era, then again in the American Founding generation.

We believe it is happening again today…"

Reader Reviews:

"Brilliant! A book on leadership written to the ultimate target audience, the leaders of the next generation! This book is not just a remake of TJEd; it's completely new material that really speaks to our current needs as parents and educators. Not only will I be recommending it to my students, but to their parents as well. What a gift to our teens, our nation and ourselves!"
– Shawn Crane, President, LEMI Mentors Association; TJEdMUSE Yahoo Group

"This a MUST READ for today's youth and their parents! Don't let the word TEENS in the title fool you. This book gives enormous perspective for all ages of people. We live in difficult times, our children have a big task ahead of them. DeMille and Brooks have prescribed usable, inspiring medicine for the maladies of our modern society and written them in a way everyone can understand."
– Nicholeen Peck, author of *Parenting a House United*

A Thomas Jefferson Education Home Companion

(with Rachel DeMille and Diann Jeppson)

At a time when the American educational system is in crisis and the family is under attack, the tried-and-true principles handed down through the ages, herein called Thomas Jefferson Education, are fostering the revival of a culture of leadership and liberty.

As a result, the family is being restored to its rightful place as the basic unit of a prosperous and free society; and the prospects for American education are looking brighter than ever.

These incredibly helpful articles read, at times, like a letter from a friend, at times like an entry in a journal of Education or Child Development, and even, at times, like we're overhearing a conversation. But in every case it is relevant, accessible, and empowering.

Visit TJEd.Org or OliverDeMille.com for more by Oliver DeMille

Leadership Education: The Phases of Learning
(with Rachel DeMille)

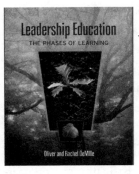

The world's problems can be summed up in just a few words: lack of leadership. While the world is in desperate need of leaders, very few people have the tools to become one.

Oliver and Rachel DeMille's Leadership Education: The Phases of Learning is the manual that every person who aspires to be an effective leader—or to raise one—needs.

Principled decision-making, the cultivation of character, studying the classics, and using critical thinking skills are just a few of the lost educational virtues of today restored by this book.

Visit TJEd.Org or OliverDeMille.com for more by Oliver DeMille

A Thomas Jefferson Education: Teaching A Generation Of Leaders For The Twenty-first Century

Is American education preparing the future leaders our nation needs or merely struggling to teach basic literacy and job skills? Without leadership education, are we settling for an inadequate system that delivers educational, industrial, governmental, and societal mediocrity?

In his flagship book, Oliver DeMille presents an overview of and a primer for an educational vision based on proven methods that really work! Teachers, students, parents, educators, legislators, leaders, and everyone who cares about our future must read this compelling book.

Reader Reviews:

"A Thomas Jefferson Education has not only helped my wife and I create a better educational environment for our children, but has constantly reminded me that master teachers believe that each child who walks into their classroom is a genius, waiting to be discovered. It's only through the efforts of educators like DeMille that we can hope to safeguard our freedom and prosperity for the next two hundred years."
– Jeff Sandefer, Founder and Faculty Member of Acton MBA

"A Thomas Jefferson Education tells us how to see, in our own day, exactly what the founders saw, and thus how to safeguard and build upon what they created. It's not a quick or painless prescription, and DeMille doesn't sugarcoat it. But he does show us, honestly and authoritatively, the price we must pay to remain a free people. If you are willing to find out what that blessing will cost you and your children, read this book."
– Andrew M. Allison, author of The Real Thomas Jefferson

"Because of this book, our home is more peaceful and the children have learned to be independently creative. Our family has developed a greater feeling of unity, and a higher awareness of God's greater purpose for our lives. To me, that's leadership training."

– Leslie Householder, Author of The Jackrabbit Factor

The Coming Aristocracy: Education and the Future of Freedom

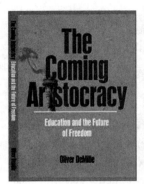

Drawing from years of intense and exhaustive research, Oliver DeMille demonstrates why social, economic, and political equality are being steadily eroded.

He highlights crucial constitutional changes, analyzes the current economic crisis, explains why both liberals and conservatives promote aristocracy, and articulates a comprehensive formula for restoring the American republic.

The Coming Aristocracy is a book for anyone concerned about the decline of America and the steady loss of freedom. More precisely, it is for those dedicated to reversing those trends through education and entrepreneurship.

Reader Reviews:

"*The Coming Aristocracy* is a clarion call for all freedom-loving Americans to awaken to our present dangers. Oliver DeMille is a modern-day Founding Father and no patriot's library is complete without this book!"
– Orrin Woodward, Best-Selling Author, *Launching a Leadership Revolution*

"Oliver DeMille arms common citizens with the knowledge, insights, and motivation they need to battle exploitation by the power and money elite. This book will help you take charge of your life and make a positive difference in these trying times."
– Mike Lathigee, Founder & CEO, Freedom Investors Club

"The Coming Aristocracy is compelling, timely, and vital. With piercing clarity, Oliver DeMille explains our current economic and political systems and resurrects the principles that made America great. Most importantly, he clearly describes what we can do as individuals, families, and communities to right our floundering ship. This may be one of the most important books you'll read this year."
– Steve D'Annunzio, Founder, The Soul Purpose Institute

ABOUT THE AUTHOR

Oliver DeMille is the author of *A Thomas Jefferson Education, The Coming Aristocracy* and other books on education and freedom. He is the founder of George Wythe University, and he has taught graduate courses on the complete writings of Thomas Jefferson, *The Federalist Papers*, Aristotle's *Politics* and other great classics of liberty. Oliver is a popular keynote speaker, writer and business consultant. Presently, he devotes a majority of his time to writing. Oliver is married to the former Rachel Pinegar. They have eight children.